SECRETS

of the
Hidden Job Market

Change Your Thinking to
Get the Job of Your Dreams

JANET WHITE

Introduction by Terry Cole-Whittaker

You're Hired! Enterprises
Plano, TX

Published by: You're Hired! Enterprises
6213 Monahans Court
Plano, TX 75023
(972) 517-7503 or (866) 563-8148
www.jobmarketsecrets.com

ISBN: 978-1-59594-052-0
    1. Self Help 2. Careers 3. Job Hunting 4. Business
    5. Metaphysics

Book cover design and photo by Leslie I. Rains
Edited by Leslie I. Rains

Printed in the United States of America

DEDICATION

To Holly and Hayden:

May you live your dreams.

ACKNOWLEDGEMENTS

This book would not have been possible without the insight, feedback and support of my editor and book midwife, Leslie Rains, who showed up in my life at exactly the right time with precisely what I needed. Leslie, I conceived this book and developed it, but you brought it into the world and graced it with your extraordinary gifts. Thank you.

I am indebted to Rev. Dr. Petra Weldes, senior minister of the Center for Spiritual Living in Dallas, and the following CSL practitioners for helping me see my Light when I was in darkness: Patti Generes, Michael Gott and Lee Wolack. To everyone at CSL who has been cheering me on as this book evolved, thank you.

Finally, I would like to thank my family, teachers and guides, bosses, colleagues and associates, all of whom contributed in some way to the formulation of the Contrarian System and my unique perspective on life. Without you, this book could never have been written.

INTRODUCTION

The common way that many people approach the job market is to think, "What should I do that will give me the money and benefits I want?" or "What is available?" so they start looking. With all those hours spent in labor to earn money, why not love what you do for a living, so that being at work is a pleasure?

The most extraordinary people you have read or heard about are those who loved their work with a passion. When you do what you love and this is your job, then you are getting paid for having a wonderful time.

Nine out of ten people lose money trying to make money, because money is not a goal, but rather a means of attaining a goal or object. The purpose of life is to give of yourself and your talents to others for their benefit. In return, you are compensated and enriched in so many ways, including financially.

You have specific natural talents that are part of your character. You will express these talents and characteristics and do what you enjoy because it is your tendency, whether you get paid for this or not.

You gravitate to those activities, so why not make them your career and life-style? A successful artist is someone who enjoys expressing through their art, and the person who buys it has an emotional attachment to the art piece. Then an exchange takes place of the art piece for money or its equivalent.

With this financial support, the artist is able to create a life-style around her passion. In this way, she can excel as she has the time to devote to the expression of her talents and also to those skills and activities she would like to develop and offer to others.

The problem with not doing your life's work is that you must support yourself in some way anyway. Think of spending an entire lifetime doing something you are either not suited for or do not like. Now contemplate the benefits of investing your life in doing work you enjoy and can pour your heart and energy into.

It is much easier for you to succeed and prosper by doing what is natural to you and what you love and you have a knack for. A person like this is called a natural, a genius, a talent, and a real treasure.

Getting up the nerve to do what you love is an important step, for unless you take this step and do it, you will never know what you are capable of attaining.

You can also do something you have never done before but have a strong interest in. Instead of looking for a job in the regular way, find out what you are truly meant to be doing.

As you use the job-finding strategy that Janet White provides in her most timely and much needed book, Secrets of the Hidden Job Market, you will soon be doing what you love and living the life-style of your choice.

Wishing you all manner of good fortune,

Terry Cole-Whittaker

TABLE OF CONTENTS

TABLE OF CONTENTS (cont.)

CHAPTER ONE

Breaking Free

*"If the shoe doesn't fit,
must we change the foot?"*

— Gloria Steinem, Author

THAT'S THE WAY I'VE ALWAYS HEARD IT SHOULD BE

*"Don't be afraid to go out on a limb.
That's where the fruit is."*

– H. Jackson Browne

Job hunting is tough, isn't it? You've looked for weeks or months on the job boards and in the want ads, go to support groups, read books that supposedly help multitudes of other people get hired, network like crazy, and email, snail mail or fax hundreds or thousands of resumes.

But nothing is happening, and you wonder what's wrong with you. This doesn't make sense. You've done everything you know to find a job, but you're still unemployed.

Or you got a job but it wasn't what you really wanted, and you had to settle for whatever you could get to bring some money in. You're all set to jump the minute something better comes along, so you go back to reading the want ads.

STOP! Searching for a job the same old way will only get you more of the same results you've been getting. If you want different results, you'll need to make some major changes – not only in what you do to get a new job, but more importantly, in what and how you think – about yourself, your employment situation and the job hunting process in general.

You may not realize it, but your thoughts, feelings and beliefs are so powerful they can help you get, or hinder you from getting, that dream job, regardless of what else you do.

No More Same-Old Same-Old

Whether you have never worked, are looking for your first job out of school or have many decades in the workforce, you have a core set of beliefs about what you have to do to get hired.

These beliefs form the job-hunting process you know, use and are convinced should work, whether it actually works for you or not. Let's call this process the "Traditional System."

But just because you believe something is true doesn't make it true in fact; it's only true in your perception, which is why it's called a "false belief."

For almost 2,000 years, people believed the earth was the center of the universe, but they didn't realize they were only at the center of their observable universe.

They assumed what they saw was all there was to see, agreed that that was how the universe worked, and couldn't accept any other possible alternative. As a job seeker, you are no different if you believe:

- You have no control over what job openings exist, which companies are hiring or who they'll pick to hire.
- You have no control over what kind of work you can get hired for.
- You have to do specific things, say certain things and act a certain way to get employers to read your resume, meet you or hire you.
- Getting hired is a matter of luck or knowing someone.
- Your potential boss calls all the shots, and all you can is wait, hope and pray.

Whether you realize it or not, your thoughts, feelings and beliefs are "manifesting," or "demonstrating" in your life all the time. For example, if you talk about how hard it is to get a good job, that's what you're going to experience because that's what you believe.

You may think you are merely commenting on a condition in your life, but you are actually creating and holding that condition in your life because you're commenting on it! In other words, it's hard for you to get a good job because you believe it is.

The good news is if you want to change your life, all you have to do is change your thinking, and your life will automatically begin to change. The bad news is that changing your thinking is not as easy as it sounds.

This book will teach you the "Contrarian System" of job hunting, which will help you change the way you think about yourself, the people you will encounter and the process of getting hired from an entirely different perspective.

Because some Contrarian System ideas may seem a bit strange at first, you may resist them. You may even get angry because they have challenged some of your core beliefs about how job hunting should be, or pushed some very sensitive buttons you didn't even know you had.

You may have years or decades invested in the Traditional System, so you may find it hard to let go of your traditional beliefs about job hunting because they won't let you go easily.

This book will teach you why it's so important for you to take charge of your thoughts, how you can intentionally change your negative thoughts to positive ones, and suggest specific actions you can take to identify and remove the barriers you are creating that are stopping your success from rushing toward you.

In every chapter, you'll find "Reality Checks" – no-holds-barred, straight-forward advice or commentary. While they may seem jarring, they are meant to help you shatter some long-held beliefs and assumptions you may be holding that are working against you.

For Recent Graduates

Congratulations on getting your degree, and welcome to the real world. As a new or soon-to-be graduate, you may have very little or no real-world work experience and few credentials, and probably expect a challenge in getting your first full-time job.

This is often the case for liberal arts majors, those in the social sciences and others who require graduate school to complete their education.

On the other hand, graduates in accounting, finance, business, engineering, science, technical or other professions often have an easier time getting hired right from school because their studies have made them "work-ready."

But if you're like most liberal arts or nontech grads, you probably have a hazy idea about what you want to do for a living, have few or no practical work skills, and turn up your nose at boring, routine and low-paying entry-level jobs.

Reality Check

Without viable work skills, you will probably only get hired for boring, entry-level jobs that pay just-over-broke salaries because you don't know enough yet to qualify for anything else.

With time and training, you can move upward and onward, but first do whatever it is you are paid to do at those dull and mind-numbing jobs. Take every chance to learn something, no matter how trivial or insignificant it may seem because it could prove invaluable one day.

At this point in your career, you'll find out very quickly how little you actually know. Keep in mind that careers aren't born and don't die with one job; they're made over time with a series of jobs in a specific industry, and you can always change your mind.

Despite what you may now believe, most people don't work in the field they majored in, don't stay with one company for a long period of time, and will switch careers at least once.

The Very Visible "Hidden Job Market"

You may have heard that a mere 15% of all currently available jobs are ever advertised and the other 85% are in the "hidden job market," whose secrets are revealed to only a chosen few.

But nothing is, or ever can be, hidden from you. In fact, everything you could want or need to get the job of your dreams is either right in front of you or is at your fingertips. It was only "hidden" from you because you couldn't see it, didn't realize it was there or didn't know how to use it.

What the Traditional System means by "hidden jobs" are those positions not advertised, publicized, posted or made available to the general public; in fact, they may not even exist yet.

In reality, companies are constantly hiring, whether or not they have formerly created a job, posted a want ad or talked about it informally. Every company has problems, and because they have problems, they need people to help solve those problems.

And because conditions affecting companies are constantly changing, the needs of companies are constantly changing. This means there is an infinite amount of employment opportunities at an unlimited number of companies all the time.

Reality Check

The only reason you will get hired is because the people hiring you believe you can help them solve their problem. Stop thinking you're "filling an opening;" you're not. You're solving a company's problem, and by solving their problem, they will solve yours.

Whether or not a job exists now is irrelevant; what matters is that a company has a problem. And since they haven't yet come up with a solution to that problem, they will hire the first person who they believe can help them solve it, which could easily be you.

A Fish Story

As a job hunter, you may feel like a salmon swimming upstream. You and hundreds of other salmon are on a quest to beat the odds and get to the top of the hill. You knew the trip would be difficult, but you never expected it to be so exhausting.

You not only have to fight the current for hundreds of miles and be constantly on the lookout for danger at every turn, but you also have to deal with intense competition for what little room there is from all the other salmon in that crowded stream right along with you.

It's a long, brutal fight against the current, so you can't ever lose focus or give up your will to win. Lots of salmon don't make it – you've known many who haven't – but you're determined to succeed, no matter how difficult it is or how many sacrifices you have to make.

You worry you won't make it before your strength gives out. You want to stop pushing yourself so hard, but you can't because others are relying on you. So, to give yourself a boost, you talk to your fellow salmon along the way.

"Don't give up," they caution. "If you get knocked down, pick yourself up and get back in the fight against the current. You have to be tough if you're going to make it."

With a sigh, you continue on, and slowly you realize that something about the stream has changed. Instead of being wide open, free-flowing and deep, the stream has narrowed, is now clogged with rocks and boulders, and the water level is shallow.

Like the other salmon, you are forced to slow down and pick your way carefully through the narrow inlets of water between the stones. What's worse, at times you find it difficult to stay completely underwater. "Oh, great," you murmur. "I'm easy pickings for whatever predator comes along. This is all I need on top of everything else."

As you wait your turn to go through a gully, hoping you'll be alive when you get on the other side, you remember a story a trout once told you. The story sounded ridiculous, but the trout was a reliable source, so maybe there's something to it.

The trout said that any salmon who breaks from the pack and swims to the shore will turn into a human being, and they could do absolutely anything they dreamed of, including getting to the top of the hill without effort.

"Could it be just that easy?" you wonder. "If the trout is right, I'd have to do something no salmon in his right mind would do – swim to the shore. I'd have to change the way I've always thought about what I have to do to get to the top of the hill.

"But if I swim to the shore, who knows what could happen? I could get caught and end up as somebody's dinner! What if there isn't enough water for me to breathe when I reach land?

"Worse of all, what if the story is made up and I'm the butt of someone's joke? If I do this crazy thing and don't turn into a human being, everyone will laugh at me. I don't want to take such a risk. That lousy trout – I never did trust him."

You're so tired and frustrated, torn about what you should do, and now you feel even worse because you're mad at the trout for suggesting such a thing. It's all too much for you, and you'd just rather give up.

But you're sick of fighting the current, you're sick of all these rocks in your way, and you're sick of the whole thing.

"Enough is enough, I've had it," you say to yourself. "I don't care what happens to me or what the other salmon think; it can't get any worse than this."

The other fish stare at you incredulously as you break from the pack and start swimming toward the riverbank. Some cynically call after you, "Just who do you think you are?" and "Where do you think you're going?" but you ignore them.

With the shoreline nearing and the ridicule of the other fish filling the water, you push yourself forward. And as your fin touches the land, to your astonishment, your real self emerges. The story was true! You're not a salmon any longer; you're a human being with the power of the Universe within you.

Incredibly, you stand upright and feel the warmth of the sun and a gentle breeze on your new body. Your gills have become lungs filled with air, your fins are arms and legs, and your scales have become skin with clothes.

Best of all, you now can see clearly straight ahead, instead of sideways through the distorted lens of water. Looking down, you see a path laid out at your feet leading through the brush away from the shore. It looks so peaceful, so natural and in a strange way, so right, as if it had been waiting for you all along.

Briefly glancing back at the salmon still fighting the current and picking their way around the rocks, you brush the branches aside and begin to walk, laughing with pleasure as the leaves crackle under your feet, the sun hits your face through the canopy of leaves overhead, and the birds chirp you a welcome.

When you were a fish, you were so busy pushing your way *through* the water that you never noticed the beauty *of* the water. The sensation of simply being alive now is incredible and you're overcome with immense joy and deep gratitude for this moment.

The incline along the path is so gradual and the journey is so pleasant that you don't realize you're making progress up the hill until your path merges briefly with the paths of other people.

These strangers are happy to see you, and gladly point out paths you didn't know about. Some paths go around the hill and have brief resting spots, others twist and turn, and some even go on to other hills, and they're all good.

Having someone help you up the hill is a new experience for you. When you were a salmon, it seemed everyone was either trying to eat you, competing against you for a position in the stream, or trying to stop you in some way because if you gained, they lost.

But these strangers, now your friends, are glad to know you. While they are helping you along your path, you are helping them along theirs in some way, even if you don't know how, so you both benefit from knowing each other.

This happens several times along your journey, and each encounter is uplifting and encouraging, moving you both along your respective paths with renewed strength and fresh insight.

And then, when you least expect it, there you are at the top of the hill – refreshed, confident, encouraged and empowered by your journey and those you've met along the way.

"This is great!" you say out loud. "I had no idea getting to the top of the hill could be so easy and enjoyable. I have to tell the other salmon!"

You rush back to the stream, shouting to the salmon: "I've discovered something wonderful. You don't have to swim against the current to get to the top of the hill anymore. All you have to do is swim to the shore!"

"Swim to the shore? Are you crazy?" the salmon cry out. "Swimming against the current is how we get to the top of the hill. This is the only way we know to get to the top of the hill! THERE IS NO OTHER WAY TO GET TO THE TOP OF THE HILL!!"

You used to think that way too, so you understand how they feel, but your experience up the hill has changed you. You now know your past is not your future, and you're not a victim of random events.

You now know you can choose your response to whatever life brings you, and that the Universe supports every one of your choices. And you know that what is true about you is also true about every other salmon, even if they don't yet know it.

It warms you to know that all salmon have within themselves an infinite number of streams and an unlimited supply of hills – each with multitudes of paths which can be joyous, fulfilling and rewarding, if they allow it.

You want all the salmon to understand that they don't have to struggle or compete for anything anymore, and that lack and limitation exist only in their minds.

And you want them to know each one of them can experience the same kind of incredible transformation you did simply by changing their thinking, so you press on.

"I know you were taught to do it that way," you say. "But if you would just trust me and swim to the shore, a whole new way of seeing life will open up before you.

"You will be able to do things you never dreamed of, have experiences you never imagined and best of all, you can get to the top of the hill without effort. I was an ordinary salmon just like you, and I did it. If I could do it, so can you."

Most of the salmon laugh at you, ignore you or shout obscenities at you. Clearly, you're insane or a troublemaker. Just who do you think you are to claim you have a better way to the top of the hill?

"Leave the safety and security of the pack in the middle of the stream and swim to the shore? Have you ever heard of anything so ridiculous?" they say to one another.

"Salmon have been swimming against the current for as long as there have been salmon. If there was a better way to get to the top of the hill, one of us would have thought of it by now."

The older salmon caution the younger ones to follow their example and play it safe: "Why take chances? Besides, whoever heard of a salmon becoming a human being? What nonsense! That person up there claiming to have been a salmon is crazy.

"Look, there are some things you just can't change. You were hatched a salmon and you'll die a salmon, so you'd better just accept it and make the best of it."

A few of the salmon pause to hear what you have to say, but the others urge them to keep on swimming. "You'll be better off forgetting that nonsense," they say. "Sure, it's tough fighting the current and trying to make headway with all these rocks in our way, but that's just the way it is.

"Getting to the top of the hill is a full-time effort, and no one ever said it was easy. If you work hard enough long enough, don't give up and have some luck, you'll have a fairly good chance of possibly making it to the top of the hill alive and in one piece. That's the best you can hope for."

With a sigh, you start to turn back toward the land, and then you see it. Out of the hundreds of salmon in that crowded stream, a few adventurous spirits have broken from the pack and are swimming toward the shore.

And as each one stands upright and begins their inward journey to their true selves, you smile.

CHAPTER TWO

Anything You Want – You Got It

"You'll see it when you believe it."

– Wayne Dyer, Author

MAKE IT SO

"Ask, and it shall be given to you."

– Jesus of Nazareth

"Be careful what you ask for because you just may get it."

– Anonymous

So, you're looking for a job; how do you feel about that? Full of adventure or terrified of rejection? Determined to nail a fabulous job or frightened you'll run out of money before you find something decent?

It may never have occurred to you, but you could be sabotaging your best efforts to get that great job right now and not even realize it.

According to quantum physics, everything in the Universe is made of energy. You are both part of and made up of this Universal energy, and you direct this energy through your conscious thoughts, feelings and beliefs.

What's more, your subconscious thoughts, hidden beliefs and long-buried feelings can be more powerful than your conscious ones and they also direct the flow of Universal energy.

The Law of Attraction

One of the immutable laws that define how the Universe works is the Law of Attraction. This law states that you draw to yourself anything you think about, focus on or believe, just like a magnet.

To see the Law of Attraction in action, take a realistic look at your life. Whether you like what you see or not, your life is reflecting back precisely what you believe to be true.

Like all Universal Laws, the Law of Attraction works exactly the same way for everyone all the time, doesn't care who uses it, has no opinion about how it is used and is entirely predictable.

You can't turn the Law of Attraction on or off, you can't get away from it, you can't deflect it and you can't minimize its effects. But when you understand that it's always working and how it works, you can harness its incredible power to change your life.

Think about soil, another Universal Law. Soil turns seeds into plants, but it doesn't care what it grows or how the seeds got there; it simply grows whatever is in the ground.

Soil doesn't judge, make decisions, set conditions, have feelings, or care what you think about it. This is why you can plant carrot seeds with absolute certainty that you will always and only get carrots from carrot seeds.

Imagine what would happen if soil was not "lawful": it might get bored of growing carrots, decide you were not entitled to carrots, get angry at you for digging that hole in it last week and grow nothing at all, or choose to grow strawberries instead.

If weeds sprouted along with your carrots, would you blame the soil? Would you beg, bargain or plead with the soil to stop growing the weeds and leave the carrots alone, fussing and fuming about the weeds choking your carrots?

Or would you resign yourself to live with the weeds, become angry that the soil is refusing to cooperate with you, or decide that you're just a victim of Mother Nature's whims?

Perhaps you could realize that since soil is simply doing what soil does, it's up to you to remove whatever weeds show up, and take action to minimize the possibility of future weeds in your garden.

Well, your mind works exactly like soil — growing the seeds of your thoughts and beliefs into "demonstrations" or "manifestations" that you can actually see and/or experience.

How you got those thoughts and beliefs doesn't matter; what

matters is that you have them, and you will inevitably see demonstrations of them one way or another.

Reality Check
Thanks to the Law of Attraction, whatever you sow, you will reap, without hesitation and regardless of whether it's in your best interest to have it. So, if you believe that dream job is already yours or if you believe you'll never get any job at all – you're right!

At the loss of a job, some people react with fear and desperation, while others cheer because they're now free to pursue other opportunities. Who do you think will have an easier time finding a great new job?

Change Your Thinking and Everything Changes
Let's say you want to be a field sales representative for Jones Manufacturing, the leader in your industry; you dream of being a sales manager someday.

As you begin to do some research on the company, you learn it has just implemented a hiring freeze which is scheduled to stay in effect for six months.

A small newspaper item gives no reason for the hiring freeze, but indicates the company is going through some internal changes. It had never occurred to you that Jones Manufacturing could be in trouble; you had always thought it was a progressive, stable company with a solid future.

Obviously, you were wrong. It's clear the company is going through a restructuring and they want to keep things hush-hush. Layoffs are next; possibly a sale. Your job hunting strategy shifts significantly as a result of this news.

You'd love to work at Jones Manufacturing if they were hiring, but since they're not, applying there would be a waste of time. But you email your resume in to Human Resources anyway – it doesn't cost you anything, and you have nothing better to do.

In a flash, it occurs to you that if Jones Manufacturing is shrinking, most every other company in the industry worth working for must be downsizing too.

With a sigh, you remind yourself how it stinks to be job hunting in such a lousy economy. You don't want to consider what an industry meltdown would do to your career.

You scour numerous job sites and find the postings for sales reps are either entry level or they want more experience than you have and are paying less than you'd settle for. It's a no-win: you're either too good or not good enough.

After weeks of intense on-line searching, you find a few positions that interest you and pay fairly decently. With a prayer, you email your resume to the Human Resource departments, hoping the companies' computers will pick up your keywords so you make it past the first screening.

Now that your search is in full swing, you join a local job hunting support group because you never know who knows somebody. You see the same people there week after week, which somehow doesn't make you feel any better, but at least it gets you out of the house.

After months of fruitless job hunting, it's obvious you are going nowhere. Clearly, no decent company is hiring field reps because you keep running into roadblocks. Most of the time, you get rejection letters or emails or no response at all.

No one returns your calls, and your few attempts at interviewing have been dismal failures. You used to be terrific at selling yourself; have you lost your touch?

Finally, you get a "Thanks, but no thanks" email from Jones Manufacturing's HR department. Well, given everything that's going on with the company and the industry, you weren't surprised.

Your family is pressuring you to forget corporate selling and get any kind of job, and you're finally beginning to agree that maybe they're right.

Out of sheer frustration and in order to pay the bills, you hang up your suit and take a job selling shoes at the mall until something better comes along.

In this example, the Law of Attraction has demonstrated that you believe:

- Job hunting is hard,
- Nothing you do works anymore,
- Your best isn't good enough, and
- Getting a decent corporate sales job is virtually impossible.

Let's make one very slight change in your thinking, which will result in an entirely different series of events. Instead of making assumptions about the implications of the hiring freeze at Jones Manufacturing, you simply take the news at face value.

The small newspaper item gives no reason for the hiring freeze, but indicates the company is going through some internal changes. This would seem to be bad news, but since you really don't know what's going on inside the company, you don't jump to any conclusions.

When you go online to do some research, you learn Jones Manufacturing's new CEO is a turnaround maven who embraces technological innovation. In a story written shortly after his arrival last year, the CEO states he plans to inject new life into this successful but weary company whose sales and stock price have gone flat.

It seems the CEO has already begun to make some changes where it counts, and your job-hunting strategy shifts significantly as a result of this news.

Even though you've never spoken to him before, you call Jones Manufacturing's Sales Director and tell him you heard about the hiring freeze, and that you know companies sometimes put hiring on hold during internal changes.

You ask him if the company is upgrading its technology, especially with the new CEO at the helm. The Sales Director is impressed you've done your homework and confirms the hiring freeze is due to a six-month-long technological overhaul of the plant, a move five years ahead of its time.

You talk with the Sales Director about the CEO's forward-thinking strategy of retooling the plant in advance of customer demand, ensuring the company's future success. You ask the Sales Director if he would give a presentation about this at the local trade group you belong to – you'll call the program chair to make the arrangements.

GooD StorY

The Sales Director is flattered and agrees, and invites you to take a tour of the plant. During the tour, it's clear that sales has taken a back seat to operations, and the current sales staff will be overwhelmed once the plant is retooled.

The Sales Director says the Chief Financial Officer imposed the hiring freeze over his strong objections, and his field staff is already swamped. His biggest concern is losing old customers in the rush to gain new ones.

At the end of the tour, you suggest working as a consultant to help coordinate the transition from old customers to new ones as the new technology is introduced, and the Sales Director asks you to prepare a proposal.

With you on board as a consultant, the Sales Director can pay you out of his own budget and doesn't have to go through the CFO, an idea he likes very much.

After several months working as a consultant for Jones Manufacturing, the Sales Director hires you as "Sales Coordination Manager," a new position just created for you. You report directly to the Sales Director, who made the CFO release the money from the corporate budget so you could be hired.

The field reps now report to you, and your bonus is based on their performance. In addition to a high salary, you have a full benefits package, your own parking spot, a two-window office with your name on the door and a secretary.

This is fantastic! You're now a sales manager and have everything you've ever dreamed of in a corporate sales job – regular hours, minimal travel, an important function that has enormous potential, a large private office, a great compensation package, and best of all, a boss who has your back. And it was all so easy!

The day you start your new job, it hits you that the company's hiring freeze is still in effect. You decide to celebrate by getting a new pair of shoes at the mall.

In this example, the Law of Attraction has demonstrated that you believe:

♦ Senior executives are easy to approach,

♦ Opportunities are everywhere when you keep an open mind,

- Getting what you want is a matter of helping someone else get what they want, and
- Life is a blast!

Affirmations Are Magic

Affirmations are seeds of energy you plant in the Universal soil – consciously or unconsciously – that grow into demonstrations. You are always affirming something:

- The economy stinks.
- No one is hiring.
- I'll never make it.
- Maybe I should just give up.
- I have to "dumb down" my resume.
- Something must be wrong with me.
- I'll never get that job.
- I'm just not good enough.
- Rejection is inevitable when you're job hunting.
- A good job hunt can take up to a year.
- I hate "selling myself."
- I can never get through.
- I'll be lucky to get anything in my field.
- I'd rather stay in this job I can't stand than look for another.
- There's too much competition.
- Looking for work is a full-time job, and no one ever said it was easy.

If this is what you're saying, then chances are, this is what you are seeing. Affirmations are extremely powerful, and you can use them to attract that great job or anything else you want into your life and keep what you don't want out of it. Here's how:

Keep Your Affirmations in the Present

The Universe doesn't know the difference between the past, present and future, so time is always "now." If you believe you already have your dream job, it will show up with minimal effort on your part because you will attract it.

It is extremely important to stay in the present and not put things in the future. When you say, "I will get a good job," you are telling the Universe that you will be gainfully employed *someday*, and your job hunt will be filled with stalls, delays and dead ends.

But if you change your affirmation to "I now have the job of my dreams," it will begin to become yours. Own it. Feel it. Embrace and embody it. Experience it as being yours now, and it will rush toward you.

Always Think Positively

Remember, negative thoughts produce negative demonstrations and positive thoughts produce positive demonstrations. So, focus only on what you want, not on what you don't want.

If you say, "I don't want to be unemployed," you are actually attracting unemployment because you're focusing on being unemployed! Instead, say, "I now have a fabulous job being paid well to do the work I love."

Move Your Feet

You must do more than just affirm what you want in order to get it; you actually have to take some sort of action, and sometimes it's as simple as just showing up.

Reality Check

When you know that the Universe will always give you what you want and you expect to receive it, you can take action absolutely confident that your "good" is already yours, even if you can't yet see it.

When I bought my house, I looked at the empty corner of my living room and said, "A seven-foot silk ficus tree belongs in that corner." I was living very frugally and refused to spend a lot of money on decorations, so I just "knew" a seven-foot silk ficus tree was in the corner and left it up the Universe to bring it to me.

Three weeks later, I was driving though the neighborhood and got the urge to follow a small sign to an estate sale. As I opened the door to the house, a branch of a seven-foot silk ficus tree selling for $20 hit my hand. It now stands in the corner of my living room.

 *I like this analogy.*

Believe It Until You See It

You can't see a seed grow in the soil, but you know it's growing anyway. And so it is with the seeds of your thoughts and beliefs. Plant your seeds of thought, allow them to grow, and trust that whatever you have asked for is on its way to you – because it is.

When you consciously, deliberately and intentionally direct the Law of Attraction, doors you thought were closed will fly open, and incredible opportunities you didn't know existed will present themselves to you.

People you never met before will come into your life, and the money and things you desire will simply show up. You'll just "happen" to be in the right place at the right time, the strangest coincidences and synchronicities will occur, and out of nowhere, that golden opportunity will fall in your lap.

No, it's not magic; it's just the Law of Attraction at work.

Post Your Affirmations Where You Will See Them

Keep your affirmations right in front of you so you constantly bombard your mind with statements of what you want: make them into screensavers; frame your computer with them, put them on your mirror, on your desktop printer and on the wall opposite your toilet; and carry them around in your wallet. You want to make sure you see them wherever you are.

Say Them Over and Over and Over

You must repeat your affirmations over and over so they sink into your subconscious until your mind habitually carries only positive thoughts and blocks any negative thoughts that may arise.

It's like learning to play the piano – you practice for hours on end to train your fingers to automatically go where they should. Once that's done, you are freed to focus on the intricacies of making music, and not on the mechanics of moving your fingers.

To neutralize habitual negative thinking, repeat your affirmations at least three times a day to get your day going right and keep it on track. Most important of all, repeat them right before you fall asleep so they sink into your subconscious.

Soon, you'll become aware when you make a negative affirmation, and then you can intentionally replace it with a positive one. Because your thoughts become your experiences through the Law of Attraction, when you change your thinking, you change your life.

Follow Your Bliss

Let's say there's something you want to do but think it's a long shot. You don't have the credentials, the experience or the contacts, and everyone tells you it's hopeless; nevertheless, that's what you want. Should you pursue it anyway? Yes, and don't let anyone tell you otherwise!

Reality Check

When you want something badly enough and believe it's already yours, the impossible becomes possible.

In the summer of my junior year of high school, I spent six weeks at a theatre workshop at Adelphi University on Long Island, and fell in love with the school. There was never any doubt in my mind that's where I would go to college.

My very realistic parents and high school guidance counselor told me to forget it. Adelphi required a minimum 85 average (I had an 80 average) and really terrific SAT scores (my scores were good but not great), and because Adelphi had their pick of outstanding applicants from all over the country, I didn't have a chance.

But I refused to listen to the "experts;" I was going to Adelphi, and that was that.

In my application essay to Adelphi, I wrote about my experience at the summer theater workshop and how I felt about going to college there; how could they resist?

When I met with the admissions director, I bubbled with enthusiasm about being back on campus and told him what a thrill it would be for me to go to school there.

And he agreed it would be a thrill to have me there.

Expect to Receive What You've Asked For

If you plant a seed in your garden and fret, "What if it doesn't grow?" or "How can I be sure it's actually growing?" you'll be digging up that seed to check on its progress and killing it in the process.

It's the same with planting seeds of thought in the Universal soil, except that your doubts, fears and negative thoughts will stop your desired "good" from manifesting, and instead, you'll get demonstrations of those doubts, fears and negative thoughts!

You see, the Law of Attraction doesn't distinguish between what you want and what you don't want; it simply creates demonstrations of whatever you think and believe.

It's very important you learn to become aware of what's going on inside your mind if you don't like what you're seeing show up in your life because what you're seeing is a direct result of what you're thinking and feeling.

Expect to receive what you have asked for, don't question or doubt the process. and be grateful that you already have received it (even if it's invisible to you at the moment). When you have accepted your good, it will rush toward you. It's really that simple.

Don't try to "make it happen." You don't need to know how what you want shows up; you just have to believe that it will . . . and it will.

Allow It to Come to You In Its Own Time

Each seed has its own internal clock: it may take weeks for a seedling to appear, months before a plant is fully grown and years before it bears fruit. You could get frustrated and impatient, insisting that the plant grow to your specifications and on your schedule.

Or you could accept that the plant knows best how, when and under what conditions it will grow, and that it will grow on its own time and in its own way, oblivious to how you feel about it.

And so it is with manifesting your dreams. The Universe knows best how to bring you what you want in the perfect way at the perfect time for you to receive it – so just release, let go and allow it to bring you your heart's desire.

Reality Check
The fastest way to manifest any desire is to think, speak and act as if it has already come true.

Suggested Affirmations

All my needs and desires are met before I even ask.

All channels are free, and all doors fly open for my immediate and endless, divinely designed supply.

All that is mine by divine right is now released and reaches me in great avalanches of abundance, under grace and in miraculous ways for everyone's highest good.

Every experience I have is perfect for my growth.

I allow myself to prosper.

I am clear on the type of work I wish to do.

I am divinely guided in everything I do.

I am financially secure.

I am grateful for all the relationships in my life.

I am grateful for all the unlimited income that flows in my life.

I am grateful for my health.

I am grateful to receive abundance and all the good in my life.

I am living my dream.

I am loved, accepted, acknowledged and appreciated.

I am a money magnet. Prosperity of every kind is mine now.

I am a powerful success magnet.

I am linked with an endless golden stream of prosperity, which comes to me in perfect ways at the perfect time for my highest good.

I am open and receptive to all avenues of income, now known and unknown to me.

I am safe and secure and financially solvent.

I am successful in everything I do.

I am surrounded by loving, giving people.

I am totally and completely supported by the Universe.

I attract a harmonious, safe and happy place to work.

I bless my bills with love and pay them promptly with joy.

I do what I love and the Universe amply supplies me.

I enjoy a steady flow of positive energy.

I freely express my creativity.

I give thanks for my new job that is a short drive from home.

I have fun while working.

I have plenty of time and money for everything I want to do.

I have the resources to develop my creative expression.

I have more than I will ever need in every area of my life.

I open myself to receive the abundance of the Universe.

I release my need for financial insecurity.

I spend money wisely and fearlessly under divine inspiration, knowing my supply is immediate and endless.

I work with compatible and balanced people.

My good comes from everywhere, everyone and everything.

My supply is endless, inexhaustible and immediate, and comes to me under grace in perfect ways.

New creative ideas come to me now.

There is no such thing as failure; only degrees of success.

CHAPTER THREE

The Trap of Tradition

*"For Sale: Parachute. Only used once,
never opened, small stain."*

– Anonymous

THE TRADITIONAL SYSTEM

You Think:
"Getting hired would solve a lot of my problems."

Your Approach Is:
Reactive – hoping something close to what you want will come along soon, but you'll take pretty much any job now.

You Use:
- A large list of companies and a catch-as-catch-can and "playing the numbers game" approach,
- A generic cover letter that pitches your qualifications,
- A jam-packed autobiographical resume showcasing your activities, achievements and attributes, and
- Wishing, hoping and pleading with God for a break.

You Work At:
- Writing, updating and polishing your resume,
- Answering want ads and job postings, contacting HR departments and recruiters, and chasing down every lead,
- Networking with everyone you know, and
- Waiting for something to happen.

You Feel:
Helpless, powerless, disillusioned, disappointed, depressed, unskilled, unwanted and unemployable.

You Subconsciously Say:
"Please hire me. I really need a job!"

THE TRADITIONAL SYSTEM:
THE WAY IT'S SUPPOSED TO WORK

*"Insanity is doing the same thing over and over
and expecting different results."*

– Albert Einstein

Of course you know how to find a job; most likely you've done it at least once in your life and probably several times. If you have never looked for a job before or need a refresher, there are thousands of websites, books and classes available.

Unfortunately, these websites, books and classes all teach you pretty much the same thing – how to work the four components of the Traditional System:

1. Networking
Traditional System networking means you talk to people who:

♦ You know and hope they know people who know people in your industry who can hire you,
♦ Know people who work for the company you want to work for so they can refer you to people there who can hire you, and
♦ Are in any company in any industry at all who can refer you to people at other companies or in other industries who might know someone who can hire you.

2. Executive Recruiters/Employment Agencies

Executive recruiters (a.k.a. headhunters) are supposed to have inside tracks to the executive suite and/or have a lock on the best jobs, and they and employment agencies are good to know because they know who is hiring and who isn't.

Besides, their job is to find jobs for job seekers, isn't it?

3. Human Resources

HR is the first hurdle to the prize of a job, as long as:

- Their computer doesn't screen out your resume,
- Your materials pitch you hard enough with the right keywords, action verbs, buzz terms and power phrases to convince them they have to hire you,
- You give all the right answers in the telephone screening interview, and
- You don't blow the face-to-face meeting.

The real issue is getting Human Resources to agree you're the ideal candidate because they decide if you're go or no-go. This can get dicey because you may never actually talk to or meet anyone from HR, so the burden of getting you to first base falls to your resume and cover letter.

If you don't make it past HR, they'll never tell you why, and you can forget a career at that company, now or ever. If you do make it past HR, you still have to meet the people who make the actual decisions, but you've been approved by HR, and they have a lot of influence with the hiring mangers about who gets hired.

4. Want Ads

A want ad is any mechanism through which anyone in the world can learn about a job opening. These include newspapers, magazines, trade or business publications, job fairs, job-posting websites like Monster.com, company websites, and on-line and offline bulletin boards.

Want ads, especially the online ones, are the backbone of the Traditional System, and you are supposed to read them daily so you can pursue every possible lead, even for jobs that aren't in your field, for which you may not have the stated qualifications, or that you could do but aren't thrilled about.

But hey, a job is a job, right?

The Traditional System: The Way It Really Works

1. Networking

Traditional System networking is based on the off chance you know someone who knows someone who knows someone who happens to be looking for someone just like you right now – and you make that connection.

In short, you are counting on other people to do your homework, open your doors, arrange your introductions, and make it easy for you to gain access to the people you want to meet, because you've convinced yourself that you're not capable of doing it.

2. Executive Recruiters/Employment Agencies

The Traditional System will have you believe that working with an executive recruiter is essential for getting one of those great corporate jobs everyone else seems to get. Nothing could be further from the truth.

Reality Check

A recruiter is not your agent, your ally or your job coach. You are not their client, and their loyalty is not with you.

Recruiters are either "inside" or "outside" a company, and each serves a specific function to corporations. What their function is to job seekers is another matter entirely.

Inside Corporate Recruiters

Inside recruiters operate as a company's in-house employment service, finding potential candidates for jobs where the turnover is typically high and the compensation is typically low, such as entry level, hourly or shift positions.

You'll see them at job fairs collecting resumes and on campus targeting graduating seniors at colleges, technical schools and graduate schools, where they are recruiting candidates for a relatively cheap labor force.

Because inside recruiters are salaried employees, they don't care which person gets hired, can't recommend who should be hired, and have no authority to hire anyone.

Outside Recruiters/Headhunters

Corporations use outside recruiters to conduct highly targeted searches for very specific mid- to upper-level executive, managerial, technical or professional positions where the turnover is exceptionally low and the compensation can be exceptionally high.

Executive recruiters are commissioned salespeople who can earn 30% to 35% of first-year compensation for the candidates they place. Their fees are always paid by their corporate clients, never by the candidates they recruit.

Because their commission depends upon making a successful placement, headhunters have a huge vested interest in making sure the "right" candidates are presented to their clients. Just as their title states, recruiters merely recruit candidates; they don't hire them.

How a Headhunter Works

As a rule of thumb, headhunters are generally not interested in anyone unemployed, self-employed or relatively unknown, and do not want unsolicited resumes from job seekers.

Nearly always, the candidates they recruit are working, and the headhunter's job is to lure them away from their current employer. If you have been recruited, you are misguided if you believe the recruiter who grooms you as a candidate represents you; they don't.

While your agenda is to get a great job with a high salary and a load of perks, their agenda is to get the deal done, take home a big, fat commission, and start work on the next deal.

Since recruiters only handle high-level or specific placements, they don't bother with anyone who doesn't fit the specifications of their search. This leaves the vast majority of job seekers to fend for themselves.

Reality Check

Executive recruiters are not in business to get you hired. Never forget you are there for the recruiter's benefit; they are not there for yours.

For a recruiter to be interested in you, you must be a highly viable candidate for a search they are conducting at that moment. Since they are only paid when they put a body in a job, they don't care whose body it is – yours or someone else's.

Employment Agencies

Employment agencies work on commission, retainer or a combination of both, and they recruit for positions that are usually skill-based. Agencies are great for filler jobs, temporary spots and "between semesters" jobs, or if all you want is any job at all that pays some bills and don't really care what kind of work you do.

The catch is you have to have the basic clerical, accounting and/or computer skills currently in demand by their clients because you're not worth anything to the agencies without them.

If you don't have these skills, many agencies will train you in the basics because the more skills you have, the more money they can make by placing you in an assignment.

Often, employment agencies will troll online resume posting boards, looking for candidates who meet the criteria of the jobs they're filling. And why not? If you have what they want and they find you, it's an easy win-win. The catch is that they have to find you.

3. Human Resources

HR has two main functions in a corporation: ensuring governmental compliance and providing services and benefits to its current and retired employees.

Hiring is not a priority in HR, is usually relegated to a junior level staffer who would rather be doing something else, and no one in the HR department has the title of "Resume Screener."

Reality Check

Human Resources has no authority to hire anyone above the level of secretary. If you are seeking any kind of managerial, executive, technical or professional position – from intern up to CEO – you should avoid Human Resources until after you have been hired, and only see them when you fill out the paperwork.

Human Resources can't hire you because HR has a "staff" function, and the hiring manager, who is a department head or corporate executive, has a "line" function. Staff always reports to line, never the other way around.

"Line" refers to the bottom line of a company's balance sheet. Line people generate and/or increase profits, save the company money and/or are in charge of those who do, and are salespeople, managers, department heads and executives. Without line people bringing in the money, there is no business.

Everyone else in the company is "staff;" instead of generating income, staff people generate expenses. Staff functions include clerical, administration, marketing/public relations, human resources, research, cafeteria, facility management, maintenance, etc.

In a layoff, staff functions are the first to be cut because a layoff has nothing to do with money; it is actually a reallocation of a company's resources – increasing line functions (income) and reducing staff functions (expenses).

This is why you will hear of companies, which are laying off staff workers and slicing or selling divisions, are simultaneously buying other companies, expanding production, hiring more line people and/or giving senior management a raise.

HR From the Inside

I once did temporary secretarial work for several weeks in the Human Resources department at the corporate headquarters of a global financial services corporation on Wall Street.

While I was there, the company was recruiting for an elite management training program that was only open to the top MBAs from the leading business schools around the country.

The HR department was astonishingly small for a global conglomerate, and the HR staff was overwhelmed with their regular work, so they had no interest in reviewing resumes for a minor corporate program that did not involve them.

As a temp, I had very little to do, so I read many of the resumes that poured in from incredibly qualified candidates, and watched as the stack of applications steadily grew untouched on a desk in an abandoned office.

Not one of these resumes was ever read, acted on or forwarded to whoever would get them next by the HR department. Finally, all the applications were all put in a box that was stored away and forgotten.

4. Want Ads

One of the big problems with reading the want ads is that it's so easy to assume the jobs you see are the only jobs available, and if you don't see a job you want, it doesn't exist.

What usually happens is that as you read the want ads, you hope and pray there will be something that has your name on it. But if you see such an ad, you can bet that several hundred other people also see that ad, and they believe it has their name on it too.

So, you send in your resume and you wait. Chances are, you'll never even get a reply or if you do, it will sound something like:

> "Thank you for sending us your resume. Unfortunately, your qualifications do not meet our requirements at this time, however, we will keep your resume on file should a suitable opening occur."

See that garbage basket near you? That's the file!

 Reality Check
The worst thing you can do when you are looking for a job is to read the want ads because it will slowly and relentlessly cause substantial damage to your self-esteem.

During this difficult time of your life, you cannot afford to constantly build up your hopes, and then get them dashed week after week, and month after month. This is why reading the want ads when you are looking for a job is the ultimate form of masochism.

So on Sunday when you get the newspaper, take out the want ads section and throw it away. Better yet, have somebody else take it out of the paper for you so you won't even be tempted to look at it, especially if there is a Traditional System career advice column in it.

And forget that Monster.com and its ilk ever existed. Don't worry; you won't be missing anything except a lot of unnecessary angst. When you stay away from the want ads and job boards, you will be amazed how much better you feel without that subliminal black cloud hanging over you. And that will make all the difference.

You Get to Be Right

Contrary to what you may now believe, the problem you have been having with the Traditional System is not how you have been doing it; you're doing it perfectly. The problem is the Traditional System itself.

Reality Check

The Traditional System of job hunting breeds a negative, self-fulfilling cycle of disappointment and disillusionment. Rather than helping you become employed and empowered, the Traditional System is designed to keep you unemployed and feeling miserable.

As you use the Traditional System, you may feel helpless, unwanted, unskilled, depressed, angry, fearful, undeserving and unemployable. You may even come to believe that you as a professional and as a person are worthless.

And here's where the Law of Attraction comes in. If you really believe nobody wants to hire you, you will find that nobody wants to hire you. And you have the Traditional System to thank for it.

Replace Negative Thinking with Positive Thinking
Without a job, I'm nothing.
My job is what I do for a living, not who I am.

My background is a jumble of job hopping.
I have a diverse range of experiences.

I don't know anyone in the industry.
I know a lot more people than I realize, and I can meet more.

Nobody wants to hire me.
The only person stopping me from succeeding is me.

No one is hiring.
Great opportunities for me are everywhere.

I've been doing this so long it's the only thing I know.
I had to learn how to do my current job, and I can learn something else. Now, what schools provide the training I want?

I don't know anyone at trade group meetings.
I am not 12 years old anymore when being shy was excusable. Besides, the whole point of my going to these meetings is to meet people, and when I do, they're not strangers any more!

What if I get a terrific job and blow it?
The only way people learn is by making mistakes, and I certainly make my share. I'm ready for more learning!

I'm too old to change.
With age comes wisdom and insight, so I'm really wise and brilliant.

I'm scared of rejection.
People have said "no" to me since I was a baby and somehow I survived. Besides, the people who say "no" to me are entitled to be wrong.

The competition's tough, and there are better qualified people than me out there looking for work.
I now accept rewarding, fulfilling and financially satisfying work perfectly suited to my personality, experience, education and expertise.

I don't know if I could make a living doing what I want, so I won't even try.

I know I could have fun doing what I enjoy, and that if I do what I love, the money will follow. I can't know how it will all turn out in the end, but there are no guarantees about anything in life. I'll just give it my best effort with high expectations that my perfect work will show up in the right way and at the right time.

I'll have to give up too much to make a career change at my age, and it will take years for me to recoup my lost income.

I'm willing to make whatever temporary life-style changes are necessary for me to pursue my dream. Besides, it won't be long before I'm up to speed in my new field making the money I desire.

No one wants to hire anyone who's been fired.

Everyone's been fired at some point, so I'm just like everyone else!

I lose every job I get.

Jobs are like relationships – just because I'm with someone for a while doesn't mean it was supposed to be forever.

What if I get fired or laid off again?

It's only a job. I'll get another.

CHAPTER FOUR

Think Contrarian

*"If your life is not going the way you want,
you can make it up differently."*

— *Terry McBride, Author*

THE CONTRARIAN SYSTEM

You Think:
"Who can I help and how can I help them?"

Your Approach Is:
Proactive – you decide what you want to do, for whom and on what terms, and take the proper actions with the conviction that your dream job is already yours.

You Use:
- A small, well-researched, detailed list of specific companies and key executives,
- A targeted cover letter tailored to each company's needs,
- A resume that presents you as a problem-solver without pitching yourself, and
- Positive affirmations, visualization and the confidence that comes with knowing your dream job is already yours, even if you can't yet see it.

You Work At:
- Mailing or emailing a limited number of letters every week to contacts on your list,
- Calling each person you contacted one week later to discuss their needs, concerns and/or opportunities, and schedule a meeting, and
- Sending proposal-like follow-up letters after the meeting.

You Feel:
Strong, confident, in control, empowered, and enthusiastic.

You Subconsciously Say:
"This company is so terrific. Let's get started!"

DIFFERENT IS BETTER

*"So go ahead and fall down.
The world looks different from the ground."*

– Oprah Winfrey

The Contrarian System is contrary or opposite to the Traditional System in just about every way. The only similarity between the two systems is that since your potential bosses don't know you, they have no opinion or are neutral about you before you contact them. And here the two systems diverge:

◆ The Traditional System assumes your potential bosses are not interested in you, which automatically moves them to "no" even before you contact them. It then becomes your responsibility to change their mind and convince, coerce or cajole them to move from "no" to "yes."

◆ But the Contrarian System assumes your potential bosses *are* interested in you, so they are already at "yes" before you contact them. As a result, the angst, anguish and turmoil that are standard fare in the Traditional System simply don't exist in the Contrarian System.

Reality Check

If you know what someone wants or needs and you help them get it, they will like you and want to know you and/or do business with you.

You have probably used the Traditional System for years and somehow gotten hired in spite of it, but it was a difficult, time-consuming, gut-wrenching and depressing experience, and you may have had to settle for whatever you could get.

That's because the Traditional System is filled with pitfalls, roadblocks and quagmires that needlessly hinder your progress, complicate otherwise simple matters, and make you feel like you're struggling against impossible odds.

Not to worry; the Traditional System helpfully teaches you how to accept, deal with, maneuver around or attempt to overcome the very problems it taught you to create for yourself in the first place!

There is another way. Welcome to the Contrarian System.

Step One: Pick Your Target

The Traditional System job-hunting sequence is like firing a shotgun; just blast away, and you'll probably hit something. Of course, what you hit may not be what you wanted to hit, and whatever you hit is now full of holes and so is everything else nearby, but no matter – you hit something.

The Contrarian System, on the other hand, is like firing a rifle. When you fire a rifle, there is one essential step you must take before you do anything else: you must first pick out a target because if you don't know what you're shooting at, nothing else you do with your rifle will matter.

Reality Check

In order to attract the job of your dreams, you must first decide precisely the kind of work you want to do, the kind of company you want to work for, on what terms you want to work, and what your compensation for that work will be. You then launch an organized, highly targeted campaign to those companies that meet your criteria.

That's right. You're going to design your own job before you even go looking for it, essentially giving the Law of Attraction precise instructions what to bring you. Affirm it, see it, and bring yourself to a place of knowing you already have it and you will.

With the conviction that comes through faith (the belief in things unseen), you can take appropriate actions toward that goal, secure in the knowledge that your dream job is already yours, even if you can't yet see it, don't have any connections, and haven't a clue how it will show up.

Are you beginning to see the difference between the Traditional and Contrarian Systems? In the Tradition System, you're trying to cram your square peg into some company's round hole, wishing and hoping that somehow you'll squeeze in.

But in the Contrarian System, you'll be attracted to companies that have square holes or that will drill a hole that fits your square peg perfectly. Getting your dream job really can be that easy.

Step Two: Do Your Homework

After you've decided what kind of work you want to do, the next step is finding companies who are doing that kind of work, and then learning as much as you can about them by using every resource you can think of, such as:

Publications and Directories

- Industry magazines to keep up with what's going on, what companies are doing what, and who the players are.
- Annual directories or buyer's guides published by trade and business magazines and associations, so you'll know who's selling what and what's new.
- Chambers of Commerce and trade associations; most of which have their membership directories on line.
- Trade show exhibitor lists, which often can be found online, so you don't even have to go to the events.
- The printed Yellow Pages, which is a giant list of local companies already sorted for you.
- Online Yellow Pages sites like www.superpages.com, which lets you search by keyword, industry and distance from your home.

Daily and Weekly Business Newspapers

♦ The news, metro and business sections of your local daily newspaper.

♦ Local or regional weekly business newspapers such as www.biz-journals.com and www.crains.com. These publications are gold mines of information, especially their annual Book of Lists, which is available in the reference section of your local library, and comes free with your subscription.

What's Right in Front of You

Let's say you're a horse lover and have been riding for years. You've never considered riding more than a hobby, and now you'd like to make a living at being around horses.

But where can you find companies in the horse business? You actually have an overload of resources, and they've been right in front of you all the time. You read the riding and breeding magazines, are a regular at the stables, haunt the western gear stores, and never miss a stock show.

There are companies in the horse business all around you and everywhere you go: they're advertising, they're being written about, you see them in the stores and online, they're sponsoring events you attend, and you're using their products.

Even though they are an intricate part of your world as a horse lover, it doesn't occur to you these companies could be potential employers because you've been waiting for them to put an ad in your local newspaper or post a listing on the job-hunting websites you cruise, which is something they may never do.

And simply because you don't see a want ad or job posting, you mistakenly conclude that companies in the horse business aren't hiring and/or don't want to hire you.

Everyone You Know In Your Industry and Those You Don't

Don't hesitate to talk to your associates, fellow employees and ex-bosses and buddies, and reach out to those you don't know or don't know well, such as your present or previous company's clients, suppliers or vendors, and especially its competitors.

You will be amazed how helpful people in your industry will be, and their suggestions can lead you in new directions and open doors you didn't even know existed. You see, you're a new source of information and contacts for them as well.

Industry Peer Groups

Don't forget trade group meetings in your area, which usually meet monthly. *This* is the networking you should be doing!

Reality Check

Regularly mingle with people with whom you want to do business and/or be affiliated because they are your potential friends, bosses, clients and colleagues. You'll get to know them and they'll get to know you, and together you'll discover ways to help each other.

You may not know anyone there yet, but don't let that stop you. Just walk up to someone, stick out your hand and say, "Hi, I'm…" The first meeting is the hardest because you have to meet new people. At the second meeting, you're seeing familiar faces, and by the third meeting, *you* are a familiar face!

Trade groups are essential for keeping up with industry trends, not only because of the peer networking, but because of the presentations and presenters. You will learn things that don't appear in the trade magazines and business press, and will make connections that otherwise may never have happened.

You can find these groups by asking people in your industry, checking at your library for a directory of associations, by going to such sites as www.weddles.com, and by reading the trade magazines in the reception areas of your company and the companies you visit.

Do a Google search for your industry, and you'll pull up trade organizations where you'll find information on your local chapter. Then just show up at the next meeting.

When you go to these meetings, you will be expected to have a business card. If you don't have a card or don't want to use the one you have, have some printed up through a local printer, office supply store or online service.

Don't go cheap and make them up on your own printer; the impression you'll make won't be worth the few dollars you'll save. Professionally printed cards will cost you about $20 for 1,000 cards and will be the best money you will ever spend.

If you're having a card printed, give yourself the title of the position you want. For example, if you want to be a fashion magazine editor, you would put on your card, "Fashion Magazine Editor." Your new title will also serve as your objective on your resume (see Chapter Seven).

Reality Check

There is no better way to attract your dream job than by seeing yourself as already having it.

Step Three: Check Your Facts

The Traditional System is a numbers game, the theory being the more companies you contact, the greater your chances of getting hired. This is why it is not unusual for a Traditional System job search to involve hundreds of companies or thousands of emails or faxes.

But since the Contrarian System works on quality not quantity, your contact list should be very short, no more than 25 companies, in fact, the shorter, the better. This list will help train your mind to envision the kind of company you'd like to work for and the type of environment you'd like to work in.

Once you have this picture in your subconscious mind, you will find that opportunities you hadn't considered or realized existed will come into your life.

Also, your list of companies is short because you're going to be spending time doing your homework on each one. Even a cursory web search will unearth a wealth of information about each company: what they do, sell or make for whom and why; the size and nature of their operation; the location of their offices and/or facilities; their position in the marketplace, and some key contacts who may or may not be relevant to you.

Do not assume any of this information is accurate or current, but use it as a starting point. Companies are constantly growing, shrinking, opening, closing, merging, moving, buying, selling, adding or dropping lines of business, hiring, firing, retiring, promoting people and restructuring themselves.

This is why any information you have gathered may be outdated by the time you see it, especially anything off the internet. Surprisingly, many company websites are updated infrequently at best.

Who Do I Talk To?

The only way to know if you have current, accurate information is to use the telephone. After verifying the company's name and address, ask the receptionist for the name and title of the person in charge of the department in which you want to work, who we will call "Mr. Bigg."

Reality Check

Mr. Bigg is the only person in this company who can hire you, and should be the only person of any authority you should be talking to, unless he refers you to another person in authority.

Everyone else you talk to should naturally be treated with courtesy and respect since they will be your colleagues if you decide to work there. That said, while some people in the company may have the ability to say "no" to you, only Mr. Bigg has the authority to say "yes," so only Mr. Bigg's opinion about you matters.

The Myth of the Difficult Receptionist

In the Traditional System, Mr. Bigg is difficult to reach:

Receptionist: "Ajax Industries. How may I direct your call?"

You: "Um, yes. I'm trying to get the name of the person in charge of your accounting department, please."

Receptionist: "I can't give out that information" or "Who's calling?" or "Is he expecting your call?"

You don't know what to say, so you mumble something about calling back later and then hang up. The infamous gatekeeper has won again.

You know you have to maneuver around this first hurdle, but Traditional System techniques about handling gatekeepers seem so phony and you don't think you could get away with them. Why do they make it so hard to get through?

Reality Check

The receptionist's job is to greet people who do business with her company and to direct their calls, not to pass judgment on them. The receptionist has absolutely no authority, can't speak for her boss or company and doesn't hire anyone.

A receptionist is not there to shield managers from unwanted intrusions, determine which calls get through, decide who is going to do business with her company, or keep strangers away from her executives like an anxious mother hen wary of a fox.

Never tell the receptionist you're looking for a job; you'll either be steered to Human Resources or be told, "We're not hiring," and you'll probably make the mistake of believing her.

And because a receptionist has no authority to ask you intrusive or interrogating questions, you are under no obligation to answer them; simply pretend you didn't hear them.

Frankly, it's none of her business what your call is about. For all she knows, you are a major customer who is thoroughly insulted at being grilled by an insubordinate clerical worker.

So, if the receptionist starts to interrogate you, pause, smile at her audacity and say it like you mean it: "I need some information. Please transfer me to accounting." Your confident manner and expectation you will be put through ensures that you will.

Step Four: You're Sherlock Holmes

Armed with this basic information about your candidate employers, your next step is to do some first-hand research about them; it's now time to play sleuth.

This extra effort can make all the difference in your job search and actually can be a lot of fun. Just think: what would be the most logical thing to do if you were a customer?

If you want to be a buyer for a fashion store chain, the most logical thing to do is to go shopping at one of their stores. As you shop, you take note of the stock, the atmosphere, the lighting, the merchandising, the background music and/or fragrance and the store layout, all from your professional perspective.

You monitor the service: is there adequate sales help or is anyone helping you at all? Does a salesperson come up to you, or do you have to find one?

If someone does help you, do they put a whole outfit together for you, or do they stand behind the counter and ask, "Did you find what you wanted?" Do they seem to care what you say?

Most importantly, you notice how you feel during your shopping experience from the minute you walk in the store to the minute you leave. Would you shop there again? Why? Why not? You can't get that kind of information sitting at home in front of a computer or by reading a catalog or industry statistics.

If you want to work for a radio station, you would get its media kit, review the ratings and listener breakdown, and listen to the station and its competitors for weeks at a time.

Assuming the formats were about the same, you would compare the on-air chatter of the disc jockeys, jingles, interaction with listeners, contests, news and cycle of play lists.

You would analyze the sound of each station for its ability to attract listeners and keep them from channel surfing. Are there any slow or dead spots? How do the disc jockeys handle goofs and mechanical breakdowns?

You would note who is advertising on each station and who isn't, what time of day and how frequently which ads run, and whether they were read live or produced in a studio.

Do the stations produce their own original programming or do they rely on syndicated or network feeds? Are you tuning in because of the disc jockeys or in spite of them?

Listen up and listen well because if you're going to work for that station, you're going to be doing a whole lot of listening to it.

Interview for Information?

The purpose of this kind of meeting is to get information about what it's like to work in that particular company or industry; not to get a job from the person you're talking to.

Requesting informational interviews is a clear sign you are inexperienced, untrained, have no viable industry contacts, and are clearly fishing. Consider these kinds of meetings only if you fall into one of these categories:

◆ College students doing an internship or term paper or who have no work-ready skills or post-graduate employment prospects lined up.

◆ Stay-at-home parents and/or homemakers and/or caretakers who have few or no skills or who have been out of the workforce so long their previous training and experiences are obsolete.

◆ Those who were fired, let go, laid off, streamlined, downsized, right-sized, involuntarily separated or were part of a "corporate profitability enhancement program," want a fresh start in a new industry, know no one and are willing to start at the bottom.

Reality Check

Informational interviews are almost always a giant waste of your time. All the information you need on entry-level jobs, starting salaries and an overview of the industry is on the web, in trade literature or at the library.

In most industries, time is money and it is unrealistic to expect to get such a time-consuming, unproductive meeting with people in any position of authority. Their time is far too valuable to sit with someone who knows nothing about their company or industry to answer such elementary questions as:

◆ On a typical day, what do you do?
◆ If you were starting over, what would you do differently?
◆ What were the keys to your career advancement?

- What are your long-range goals?
- What's the corporate culture like here?
- What values are important to your team?
- What obligation does your work put on you outside the work week? How much flexibility do you have in terms of dress, work hours, vacations?
- What problems does the organization as a whole have? What is being done to solve these problems?
- Is there a typical chain of command in this field?
- What trends do you see for this industry in the next three to five years? What kind of future do you see for this organization?
- What are the most important personal satisfactions and dissatisfactions connected with this occupation?
- What do you expect of people starting out in this field?
- What personal qualities are needed to succeed in this line of work?
- What are some of the ways I can become familiar with the industry's jargon?

Reality Check

If you are experienced and just changing jobs within an industry, you will have questions that won't be answered in an informational interview because most people are extremely reluctant to talk about sensitive company issues in their office.

Besides, you probably won't be meeting with anyone willing or able to tell you what you really need to know, like:

- Why was that new line cancelled at the last minute?

- Rumor has it that the president of the firm you acquired that became your new networking division was a convicted forger out on probation. It's a good thing you didn't hire him; how did you find out the truth?

- There's talk the company is thinking of relocating its headquarters so the CEO can go fishing at the lake where he grew up. Are you going to go?

- With this company going public in a few years, there will probably be pressure to drive sales to inflate the company's value to Wall Street. How will the sales quotas be affected, and how will the company support the sales force in meeting those numbers?

- What are these ridiculous gas prices doing to your profit margin? How will they impact your plans to expand?

Reality Check

The best way to get information about the inner workings of the companies you're interested in is to speak to friends, colleagues or clients, and especially salespeople who work for or with those firms. This is why memberships in industry trade groups and relationships with peers are so valuable; you never know who may know who or what they know.

You want these meetings to be off the premises and as informal, low-key and relaxed as possible, preferably over drinks or a meal. Once you two become friends or at least casual business acquaintances, you'll find getting "inside" information and making other connections a whole lot easier.

CHAPTER FIVE

Be Afraid . . . Be Very Afraid

"The University of Illinois hired fifteen women to smell pig manure so researchers can learn what makes pig manure smell so bad.

You know who I feel sorry for? The women who applied for this job and got turned down."

— Jay Leno, Talk Show Host

IN SEARCH OF THE HOLY GRAIL

"You can have everything in life you want, if you will just help other people get what they want."

– Zig Ziglar

The Traditional System puts such a tremendous amount of importance on your resume that you may be concerned that yours is not perfect, and you have every reason to be concerned.

According to the Traditional System, if your resume has one awkward statement, the wrong keywords, not enough power phrases, is in the wrong format or has an unacceptable font, you are doomed to a lifetime of bad jobs or chronic unemployment, with "Failure" stamped across your resume for all to see.

And the vast majority of online resume-writing services make sure you realize your dilemma is entirely your own fault for not hiring them. This website pulls no punches:

"Whether you want to face it or not, this is a contest. You might be the best candidate, and you might be the most qualified.

"But if you don't make your resume stand out from the rest – if you don't make the right first impression – you'll never land that interview. And if you never land that interview, that job of your dreams is just a dream.

"Your resume is one of the most important documents of your life.

"Your resume is your calling card, your best chance to make a first impression.

"Without an exceptional resume, you won't stand a chance of standing out from the crowd and landing those interviews you need.

"Our job is to get you interviews. Our job is to sell your skills and your experience in the most professional and convincing way.

"The old adage is absolutely true: your resume has to capture your reader's attention within ten seconds. If the reader is not impressed, then what's to stop them from moving on to the next resume in their files?

"We know how to make you stand out. In a situation when you need to be absolutely sure of quality, don't leave your future to chance. Trust it to professionals. You need to stand out. Do you know how to do that? Do you know how to sell yourself effectively?

"Do you know how to add the right keywords so that your resume will be found in resume databases?

"Do you know how to design a winning, eye-catching document?

"Do you know the proper resume format for your career?

"Do you know the resume format Human Resource professionals prefer?"

The hype on this website and so many others is intentionally designed to part you from your money through fear-based, hard-sell tactics and proclamations of doom about what might happen to you if you don't hire them.

Reality Check

Every implication that you are unable to get the job of your dreams all by yourself is totally, completely and absolutely wrong.

Let's take a clearheaded, rational look at their claims through the lens of common sense, sound business judgment and an understanding of basic human psychology:

> "Whether you want to face it or not, this is a contest. You might be the best candidate. You might be the most qualified.
>
> "But if you don't make your resume stand out from the rest – if you don't make the right first impression – you'll never land that interview. And if you never land that interview, that job of your dreams is just a dream."

The premise for this argument is if you don't have a superior resume (i.e., one that is written by them), you won't get the interview that will get you hired. If you accept this line of thinking, you may also believe:

- You're competing with multitudes of other similarly qualified people for the same job,
- There is a lone individual in Human Resources who shuffles the stack of resumes like a deck of cards and who has the sole ability and authority to deal you in or out, and
- The only thing that differentiates you from everyone else in that stack is how your resume is written.

None of these statements are really true, but if you believe them, they will be true for you, and you will experience them through the Law of Attraction.

> "Your resume is one of the most important documents of your life."

Your resume is important when you're job hunting, but it's not nearly as important as your cover letter. While an effective cover letter can open doors even without a resume, your resume on its own won't get you an interview and it won't get you hired.

It is also a real stretch to call a resume "one of the most important documents of your life" because you may have many resumes over your career, and perhaps different resumes for different companies in the same industry at the same time.

In fact, a resume doesn't even rate next to genuinely important documents like your birth certificate, diploma, passport, mortgage, driver's license, marriage license, bank statements, credit reports, school records, military discharge papers, etc.

> "Your resume is your calling card, your best chance to make a first impression."

Since no one in the 21st century uses a real calling card, it's possible the writers of this site have confused a resume with a relic of 19th century etiquette.

Before there were telephones, emails and instant messages, people "called" or visited each other each other if they wanted to chat, leaving "calling cards" if no one was home. So, calling cards and resumes have absolutely no connection with each other.

> "Without an exceptional resume, you won't stand a chance of standing out from the crowd and landing those interviews you need."

This goes back to the job-hunting-as-contest scenario in which your resume must fight to be noticed amidst a sea of equally outstanding resumes. It also implies your resume alone will or won't get you an interview, another false belief.

> "Our job is to get you interviews. Our job is to sell your skills and your experience in the most professional and convincing way."

This statement might be true only if the resume company was paid if and when you landed a face-to-face interview as a direct result of their work. Since they do not work on contingency and do not arrange interviews for job seekers, their claim is patently false.

"The old adage is absolutely true: your resume has to capture your reader's attention within ten seconds."

This false belief is one of the cornerstones of the Traditional System: your resume, your career – you – are being judged by a total stranger in a mere ten seconds, and this person has the sole authority to decide if you are worthy to begin the process of being selected to be considered to be hired.

"If the reader is not impressed, then what's to stop them from moving on to the next resume in their files?"

If you try to impress the reader by telling them what a superbly talented and skilled proven performer you are, they *will* move on to the next resume, which is also trying to impress the reader how that candidate is also a superbly talented and skilled proven performer.

"We know how to make you stand out. In a situation when you need to be absolutely sure of quality, don't leave your future to chance. Trust it to professionals. You need to stand out. Do you know how to do that? Do you know how to sell yourself effectively?"

Of course you don't. Why should you? "Selling yourself" is unnatural behavior. Think about it – do you know anyone who is an expert at selling themselves?

Pitching and hustling are fine if you're selling a whiz-bang at the county fair, but they are never appropriate in business. They also never work if you're trying to get someone to like you because being forceful and boasting about yourself alienates the very people you want to attract.

"Do you know how to add the right keywords so that your resume will be found in resume databases?"

This question assumes your resume will be scanned by a computer before human eyes ever see it, and that the computer decides who makes the initial cut based upon the words it finds.

The problem is that the computer doesn't have the faintest idea what those words mean; all it does is scan for the words it was programmed to find.

Reality Check

Electronic/scannable resumes are written to be read by a computer. But you will not be hired by a computer; you will be hired by an intelligent human being with two eyes, a brain and feelings and who uses all of them all of the time.

When you submit an electronic or scannable resume to a company's database, you are allowing a machine to come between you and the job you want.

"Do you know how to design a winning, eye-catching document?"

The only people who should care about designing winning, eye-catching documents are those who compete in resume design competitions, if such things exist. The design of your resume is irrelevant; the only things that matter are what your resume says and how Mr. Bigg feels as he reads it.

"Do you know the proper resume format for your career?"

Since when are there "proper resume formats" for each career, who made such a decision and where is the list?

"Do you know the resume format Human Resource professionals prefer?"

According to CareerJournal.com, (the career advice website from the Wall Street Journal), the resume format most HR professionals prefer is the chronological format. According to Monster.com, the resume format HR professionals prefer is the functional format.

So flip a coin and take your pick. These "experts" don't know any more about resume formats than you do. Here's a review of both these formats from CareerJournal.com:

The Chronological Resume
"Its name a misnomer, the chronological resume presents work experience in reverse-chronological order so that your current or most recent employer is listed first.

"Information is organized so that a reviewer can scan the document and quickly gain a good understanding of your career progression, including the types of companies you've worked for, dates of employment, job titles and, most important, your responsibilities and accomplishments."

The Functional Resume
"Functional resumes discuss work experience according to functional strengths, not by employers. The emphasis is on what someone has done, not where and when the work was done.

"This enables a job hunter to immediately highlight certain talents and accomplishments, while concealing the types of liabilities the chronological format would showcase."

Uh, I Can Explain That
Whoa! What was that again? CareerJournal.com continues:

"Unless you have an unblemished background, a resume isn't the perfect device for presenting work experience. In fact, the greater the number of liabilities a job hunter has, the less this document can be relied upon for producing interviews.

"This is especially the case when responding to internet postings, answering ads or conducting a mass mailing to prospective employers or recruiters. In these cases, you'll face formidable competition from job hunters whose resumes contain no background deficiencies."

Uh, oh. Now you're in big trouble. It's bad enough you have to have the right keywords, action verbs and layout so you can pitch yourself to nameless, faceless strangers who have the authority to pass judgment on you and decide your fate in ten seconds.

But now you have to worry about having – or worse, being perceived as having – what CareerJournal.com calls "red flags, blemishes, liabilities and deficiencies" like "employment gaps, job performance problems or personal and other issues which may scare off an employer and should be omitted or disguised."

Perhaps you were laid off, fired or quit. Maybe you took time off to be with your family, serve in the military, get or complete a degree, recover from an illness or accident, start a business, enjoy early retirement, explore a new line of work or take a well-deserved personal sabbatical.

But according to the Traditional System, if you've had any kind of a life at all, you have some major obstacles to overcome, and you lose no matter which way you turn:

◆ Are you a job hopper or did you stay in one job too long?
◆ Have you been job hunting too long or are you jumping too soon?
◆ Do you have too much experience or not enough?
◆ Are you over educated or under trained?
◆ Have you been promoted too quickly or not at all?
◆ Are you leaving your current employer because you've gone as far as you can or because you refuse to fit in?
◆ Is your experience too general or too specialized?
◆ Did you chase after rainbows or get stuck in a rut?
◆ Did you go to the right school or some place no one ever heard of?
◆ Did you take classes to make yourself employable or did you follow your passion?
◆ Did you work from home, experiment with self-employment or simply not work at all for a while, and are now carrying the stigma of "returning to the workforce"?
◆ Have you relocated too much or stayed put?
◆ Was your graduation too long ago or too recent?
◆ And what about your age?

It's All Good

Regardless how much or how little experience, education or expertise you have, you are the best you can be right here, right now, and you are in Day One of the rest of your life.

You can't redo the past, so it's a waste of time to look back. What you did or didn't do then is irrelevant; what matters is what you plan to do now and going forward.

There is no need to feel defensive, apologetic or that you are somehow "not enough." You are a perfect creation of a perfect Universe, and you can't get any more "enough" than that.

Purge yourself of any sense of inadequacy brought on by the Traditional System or anyone or anything else. These negative feelings aren't doing you any good, so get rid of them.

Instead, use positive affirmations, creative visualization and proper actions to direct the Law of Attraction to bring your heart's desire to you.

And you will find that no one's opinion about you matters, except your own.

CHAPTER SIX

You, Only Better

*"Whenever you are asked if you can do a job,
tell 'em: 'Certainly I can!'*

Then get busy and find out how to do it."

*— Theodore Roosevelt,
Twenty-sixth President of the United States*

FOR THEIR EYES ONLY

"Writing is a socially acceptable form of schizophrenia."

– E.L. Doctorow

As you begin to apply the Contrarian System, you'll not only understand why your Traditional System resume isn't working for you, but how it is probably working against you. To start, there are only two Contrarian rules of resume writing:

Rule #1:
Write Your Resume from Mr. Bigg's Perspective
As he reads your resume, Mr. Bigg is thinking:

◆ Who are you?
◆ What have you done?
◆ For whom have you done it?
◆ Why should I care?

And you can believe that "Why should I care?" is more important than everything else put together. Mr. Bigg may carry the title of CEO and run a multi-billion-dollar corporation, but he's still his kids' dad, his wife's husband and his mom's son.

Mr. Bigg was a kid himself once and has a family, friends, hobbies, religious convictions, health concerns, a cultural heritage and his own peculiar quirks, interests and passions inside and outside of work.

If you can get past all the corporate hoopla, you'll find that Mr. Bigg is just a regular guy. He has no "off" button; he is not a machine, in fact, in many ways, Mr. Bigg is just like you. He thinks, feels and responds to situations a lot like you do because you both are people, and people are extremely predictable most of the time.

Like you, Mr. Bigg throws out junk mail, ignores anyone who tries to sell him something he's not interested in buying, and knows when he's being snowed. He makes decisions based on what he thinks combined with how he feels, and while he listens to the opinions of others, he makes his own decisions, which is why he's the boss.

Reality Check

Mr. Bigg is the center of his own universe and has a life, and anything that makes his life better makes him feel good, something he very much likes to have happen.

Mr. Bigg is not interested in your accolades, accomplishments or action verbs, so telling him how wonderful you think you are will only backfire. He does not care about what you want; all he cares about is what he wants. And if you can help him get what he wants, he will help you get what you want.

Rule #2:
Write in English, not "Resume-Speak"

Don't turn plain, ordinary, conversational English into incomprehensible gobbledygook! Traditional System resumes are notorious for using convoluted language when very simple words will do. Here's an excerpt from a senior level marketer's resume:

> "Driver and champion of transformational programs – able to gain executive sponsorship, build internal support at all levels and create cross-functional project teams that deliver exceptional results."

"Expert in aligning strategy with organizational vision and goals and interpreting the voice of the customer through enhanced insight and knowledge management."

Or this one from a technology manager:

"Record of focused, growth-oriented, strategic leadership that boosts profitability, speeds time to market, reverses poor financial performance, and drives progress for start-up, early-stage, high-growth and emerging technology companies.

"Strong executive-leadership competencies in all areas of the organization; talent for identifying strategy, communicating vision, developing tactical plans and motivating and empowering teams and individuals to achieve remarkable goals."

Or this one from a new college graduate:

"Consistently offer an energetic and enthusiastic approach to projects and assignments, as well as a thorough understanding of the importance of time management and personal organization.

"Proven ability to analyze consumer markets based on financial data, consumer trends and company structure to effectively direct resources in order to gain market share."

Reality Check

You can make your resume inviting to read and easy to understand by writing the way you talk in normal conversation.

If you hold the Traditional System belief that you have to move Mr. Bigg from "no" to "yes" by "selling yourself," it may be challenging for you to write in plain, simple English at first.

Keep in mind that you're now in the Contrarian System, and because Mr. Bigg is already at "yes," he doesn't need to be impressed or convinced of anything. He just wants to know more about you, and he will instinctively resist you if you "sell yourself" to him.

In the following sections and chapters, you'll find numerous examples of how Traditional System resume-speak can be easily turned into ordinary English in your resume and cover letter.

But remember, it's not so much the words you use as the feelings you put behind them because Mr. Bigg will respond with feelings of his own.

Debunking Resume Myths

The Traditional System is infused with numerous myths about resumes. Here are the big eight:

Debunked Resume Myth #1:
Your Resume Is Your Big Ticket To Getting Hired

The Traditional System is adamant that the sole purpose of your resume is to get you that all-important meeting because if you don't get that meeting, you'll never get hired.

Reality Check

The purpose of your resume and cover letter is to start a conversation with someone you think you might like to work with or for. A meeting may not be necessary for that to happen.

In the Traditional System, your resume is very complicated and your cover letter is very simple; it's usually just a transmittal device for your resume. In its most common form, the cover letter is a "son of resume" with a pitch for a meeting.

But in the Contrarian System, your resume is very simple; it's the cover letter that is complicated. To do it right, you have to write your letter as if you were Mr. Bigg and were reading it for the first time (see Chapter Nine).

Although your cover letter is much more important than your resume, it will be easier for you to understand and apply Contrarian System concepts if you work on your resume first, so don't jump ahead just yet.

Debunked Resume Myth #2:
There is a "Perfect" Resume

Deep within the Traditional System is the myth that someone, somewhere, has a magical mixture of action verbs, power phrases, keywords and layout that will fill an employer with desire to meet you. No one has ever found this elusive resume formula simply because it doesn't exist.

Reality Check
The only reason Mr. Bigg will want to know you is because he believes you may be able to help him solve a problem or fill a need he has.

Webster's Dictionary defines a resume as "a short account of one's career and qualifications prepared typically by an applicant for a position."

The Traditional System says your resume is a professional autobiography detailing your job history, career moves, capabilities and accomplishments. It also serves as your advertisement because it tells your story, makes your pitch and is "you" to the world.

Reality Check
Your resume is a finely crafted sales tool, and *you* are the product it is representing.

You're a Copywriter

Imagine you're breezing though the lawn-and-garden section of your local home improvement store when you see a brochure for a new kind of lawn mower. See that brochure in your mind and focus on the text.

The copy is easy and pleasant to read, and gives you tips how this new lawn mower will help you care for your lawn while lowering your costs and giving you more free time.

A great deal of research about homeowners like you who do their own yard work went into the writing of that brochure, so it's no accident you can relate to it.

You haven't noticed it, but that brochure has given you just enough information to get you interested in that lawn mower: how it works, why it's different from other lawn mowers and why you should care about it.

But a lot has been intentionally left out. You were not told how the lawn mower was developed, or that its technology required years of work from teams of lawn mower developers, or how proud the company is of its new baby.

And what's also missing is the hype. If the brochure told you this was the best lawn mower on the planet, would transform your yard into a paradise or was the answer to your lawn mower prayers, you would instinctively feel you were being pressured or hoodwinked and throw the brochure away.

Instead, the brochure is a fast, easy, informative and enjoyable read, and when you're done, you'll probably want to take a closer look at that gleaming model on the showroom floor.

And that was exactly what was supposed to happen. That little brochure has moved you from being neutral about buying that new lawn mower to being on the way to a "yes," and you never once felt you were being sold; you were buying.

Well, your resume is your brochure, written for Mr. Bigg in his language, giving him just enough information about what he is interested in to move him to the next step – meeting you.

Reality Check
Your resume is an introduction to you with the intent that a relationship of some sort with Mr. Bigg will develop over time.

Your resume is an appetizer, a sampling, a flavor of you as a professional, a taste of what you have to offer; it is not an eight-course meal. Put too much information on your resume and you will give Mr. Bigg indigestion.

Debunked Resume Myth #3:
Rewriting is Unnecessary
Another myth of The Traditional System is once your resume has been written, it can never be changed; it can only be "updated" or "polished" with each job change. You must stop believing your resume is cast in stone forever and all time, regardless of how much

work you have put into it or how much you have paid someone to write it for you.

Reality Check

Your resume should be reviewed, revised and reworked as often as necessary so that it accurately portrays you the way you want Mr. Bigg to see you, which is not necessarily the way you are. This is why your resume is a sales tool and not an advertisement.

You may have heard the adage, "Dress for the job you want." Since you only get one chance to make a first impression, you use clothing to project an image of you as a person who already has the position you desire. Well, you can do precisely the same thing with your resume.

This is possible whether you're just starting out or are a seasoned veteran with many years of experience under your belt. Here's how I described my first job in commercial real estate:

"As a staff member of Mall Properties, Inc., I was involved in all phases of the firm's development activities – from project conception, land assemblage, financing and regulatory approvals, through construction, leasing and management.

"I assisted in the development and preleasing of a regional mall in Connecticut with major environmental issues, and the marketing of a luxury residential subdivision in Pennsylvania."

Sounds impressive, doesn't it? Read it again – what was my job? What did I actually *do*?

The truth is that I was the secretary for the executive vice president of real estate development, and my job was to type his letters, file his papers and answer his phone. For the two years I was with that company, my sole "accomplishment" was reorganizing its filing system.

But you would never know that because I didn't see myself as a secretary; I saw myself as a junior professional in commercial real estate who worked on some nifty projects, which is how I wanted my future bosses to see me (see Chapter Eight).

Notice that I didn't lie, stretch the truth or pretend to be something I wasn't. On the contrary, everything I put on my resume was absolutely accurate, truthful and provable:

- I *was* a staff member at Mall Properties.
- I *was* involved in all phases of the firm's development activities. As the secretary to the executive vice president of development, naturally, I would be.
- I *did* assist in the development and preleasing of a regional mall in Connecticut with major environmental issues, and the marketing of that residential subdivision. I considered typing, filing and answering the phone to be "assisting."

And I could discuss that regional mall and its environmental problems in depth because I read every piece of paper in every single file while I cleaned up the filing system.

It took months to go through the drafts of leases and correspondence about land acquisitions, project financing and lease negotiations with the department stores and mall tenants, and it was amazing what I learned:

- There were legions of correspondence over the land-use hassles with the Army Corps of Engineers, which chose to conduct its site inspection the day a hurricane hit the area. To the developer's chagrin, the Corps promptly declared the development site to be federally protected wetlands.

- Simultaneously, the nearby town had very legitimate concerns that the mall would decimate its already struggling Main Street, so it too was battling the developer, who was determined to get this property built regardless of how the community felt about it.

- To answer his critics and satisfy federal law, the developer hired a consultant to prepare an environmental impact statement about the project, whose findings were (no surprise) favorable to the developer.

WHAT GOES IN YOUR RESUME

Objective
What you want

Experience
What you've done and for whom

Education
What you've learned and where

Other Information
Industry organizations you belong to,
recognitions or honors you've earned,
other information relevant to your objective

What Stays out of Your Resume
Everything else!

As a result of this routine clerical chore, I got a priceless, hands-on, real-world education about the realities of big-time commercial real estate development, an invaluable gift to an industry wannabe.

Rather than being an autobiographic work history, my resume was a finely crafted sales tool that projected me precisely the way I wanted to be seen – as a knowledgeable junior industry professional, not as a smart, ambitious secretary yearning to be on the other side of the keyboard.

In case you're wondering, throughout my subsequent 18 years in commercial real estate, no one ever doubted, questioned or inquired what I actually did at Mall Properties. It simply didn't matter.

Debunked Resume Myth #4:
You Don't Need an Objective
It's not just important to have an objective; it's absolutely critical you have one in order to get the job you want.

Reality Check ✔

Your objective is first on your resume because it's the most important thing on it.

Your objective has two core functions:

- It serves as a unifying force for your resume – put in your resume everything and anything that relates to, fulfills or supports your objective, and leave out everything else.

- It states what you want and what you expect to receive. Without an objective, your resume defaults to being an autobiographic work history, and Mr. Bigg is forced to guess what you want and what you want to do for him. Do you really think he will?

Are You Impressed Yet?

Some Traditional System pundits urge you to use a summary of qualifications instead of, or in addition to, your objective. The rationale is since you only have ten seconds to wow 'em, you'd better do it big, loud and right up front. One resume website defines a summary of qualifications as:

". . . a short statement that highlights your abilities and facilitates the 'high-speed resume scanning' that Human Resources personnel have to do."

The proponents of summaries of qualifications say you need to make a fast, strong impression. Oh, you'll make a fast, strong impression all right, but not the one you want to make.

Let's say you're meeting someone for the first time and in order to impress you, they spend the whole time talking about themselves. Your instinctive response to this self-centered individual is to decide to never intentionally be with them again.

Reality Check

Instead of opening doors, your summary of qualifications is putting a wall between you and Mr. Bigg. You are literally repelling him when you tell him how wonderful you think you are, and the more you talk about yourself, the less likely he is to like you.

As you read the following summaries of qualifications, keep in mind that what you feel about these candidates is precisely what Mr. Bigg feels about you when you say much the same things about yourself:

"A flexible, results-oriented team player with excellent communication, problem-solving, computer, leadership and organizational skills. A proven ability in ambiguous, multi-disciplined settings."

"Experienced problem-solver with demonstrated ability to perform critical analysis and take responsibility for project success. Proven record of pro-active leadership and collaboration."

"Intricately seasoned manager and 'business connoisseur' with a polished history of utilizing word-of-mouth advertising for longevity, while incorporating diverse medias, unique marketing strategies and a no-questions-asked service department."

"Results-oriented, visionary leader with a strong track record of performance in multi-channel (store, catalog, and e-commerce) retail business. Utilize keen analysis, insights and team approach to drive organizational improvements and implementation of best practices. Superior interpersonal skills, capable of resolving multiple and complex (sales, human resources, legal, financial, operational) issues and motivating staff to peak performance."

"Achieved 'impossible' performance improvements in demanding industries by clearly communicating vision, instilling team culture, and igniting competitive drive."

Isn't it obvious that these people are trying really hard to make an impression? Unfortunately, the only impression they're making is that they're full of themselves. If you were Mr. Bigg, would you want such a self-involved egotist on your team?

I'm All Grown Up Now

The Traditional System advises you new graduates to use a personal profile in lieu of a summary, since you don't have many or any professional qualifications to boast or brag about. Instead, you're supposed to boast or brag about yourself, like these grads do:

"Highly flexible, adaptable performer; adept at multi-tasking and thriving in a fast-paced environment while coordinating numerous time-sensitive projects. Exceptionally motivated self-starter and creative problem-solver who works hard and loves a challenge."

"Excellent organizer with solid planning and problem-solving skills. A self-starter who can work independently and handle multiple priorities and deadlines. A quick learner who rapidly masters all aspects of a job with limited training."

"A high-energy, self-motivated team player with accurate, professional nature; requires minimal supervision. Able to work under pressure, handle multiple demands and set priorities. Excellent public speaking and communication skills."

"Genuine talent in building trust relationships, communicating across all age groups and levels of an organization. Excellent qualifications in leadership, customer relationship management and employee supervision and training."

"Record of new business development in unfamiliar industries. Sincere and empathetic, with a client-focused approach fostering trust and allegiance. Quickly climbs to leadership roles with ability to teach newcomers."

Reality Check

If you are new to the workforce, you simply cannot fake real-world experience you lack, training and insight into the nuances of your industry you don't have, or a history of performance that doesn't exist.

It is extremely unlikely that the 22-year-old college senior who wrote the following Traditional System personal profile really is what he claims to be, considering he's looking for his first full-time job:

"Motivated team player with demonstrated talent for deploying research and organizational skills toward analyzing, upgrading and streamlining complex marketing processes for improvement opportunities.

"A goal-driven achiever with strong organizational skills and an orientation to detail. Enthusiastic self-starter who can boost productivity, cut costs, foster efficiency and ensure profitability to an organization."

Why Should You Hire Me?

It's the eternal Catch 22: how can you get a good job to gain experience unless you've had experience? The solution is to get the skills companies want, and be willing to learn the business from the ground up. Every professional worth their salt has to pay their dues by starting at the bottom, and it's now your turn.

Reality Check

Mr. Bigg will expect you to start earning your pay from Day One, and he will hire you because of what you can do, not because of who you are. In other words, you will be hired because you are already trained in the fundamentals of your work, not because you are trainable.

If you're a typical college undergraduate in your early 20's, you probably have a vague notion of what the real world of working full time is like, even if you worked part time or did internships.

For the real skinny about what you need for entry level – or any level – jobs in any profession, go to the U.S. Department of Labor's website at www.bls.gov.

The Pre-Job Job

By all means, pursue all possible internships while you're in college, but don't expect them to lead to a job offer. That's not their purpose. Internships give you something to put on your resume, and offer insight into a profession so you can decide if it's for you or not.

I had such an experience when I was a reporter intern at News-day during my sophomore year in college. I was one of ten college students selected from a pool of 1,500 applicants from all over the country, and worked in the City Room in the newspaper's main Garden City, Long island offices.

This was long before word processing and PCs, so we wrote our stories on manual typewriters using tripled carbon paper. Between the clacking of typewriter keys, the constant muted humming of the newswire machines in an adjacent room, and the chatter of thirty or so reporters all talking on headsets, it was a fabulous place to play reporter. And they paid me to work there!

My formal "training" at Newsday consisted of the day editor having me rewrite my first story nine times with such instructions as "Tighten up the ending," and "Make the middle flow better." Oddly enough, I knew what he meant.

During my four months at Newsday, I wrote numerous two-paragraph filler items and several by-line features, including a story about ducks dying at area ponds. "Give me a thousand words," my editor said. I did. I also wrote about a dozen obituaries a day.

It sounds gruesome, but writing those obituaries taught me very quickly the fundamentals of reporting: the necessity of verifying a death with the funeral home, how to interview family members (most of whom were thrilled that a story was being written about their loved one), and most importantly, how to pack information about the deceased's life into a short, easy-to-read, solid news story – without fluff, judgment or emotion.

My stint at Newsday taught me that reporting wasn't in my blood, but years later, I would become a professional business writer using the exact same techniques to put together articles and press releases as I did writing all those obituaries and news stories.

So, how does this jive with the Law of Attraction? Having a strong belief in what you can do is essential to attracting your dream job, but that belief is strengthened when you actually have the ability to do that job. After all, why would you want a job you couldn't do, weren't interested in or didn't like?

Starter Jobs

There is a Traditional System myth about the plethora of entry-level training corporate programs for new graduates. Such programs do exist at some companies, but they are few, far between and usually limited to technical, engineering, scientific research, business and sales positions, or are for post-graduates with specialized training and/or experience.

Getting your first few starter jobs after college will be a whole lot easier if you already have work-ready skills that companies need. If you don't have such skills, you will probably have to take classes at a community college or trade school to supplement your degree or take classes at night during your senior year of college.

Then you'll be ready to be out on your own by the time graduation rolls around because you'll be able to support yourself independently as an adult. As a result, your transition from college to the real world will be a joy instead of an ordeal.

If you get your supplemental career training after you've graduated, you can work at one of those just-over-broke jobs you didn't go to college for while you're learning the skills you didn't go to college for so you can get one of those jobs you went to college for.

New graduates, congratulations on getting your degree. Your education has just begun.

CHAPTER SEVEN

Telling Your Story

"I have missed more than 9,000 shots and lost almost 300 games in my career.

On 26 occasions, I was entrusted with the game-winning shot . . . and missed.

I have failed over and over and over again in my life, and that's precisely why I succeed."

– Michael Jordan, Basketball Player

I AM . . . I SAID

*"Even if you're on the right track,
you'll get run over if you just sit there."*

– Will Rogers

Debunked Resume Myth #5:
Having an Objective Limits Your Options
Actually, having an objective broadens your options because it forces you to focus, and when you focus, you can identify opportunities you probably never would have thought of. Let's say you want to sell commercial air time for a local radio station. But you could:

- Sell commercial air time for unaffiliated, independent radio stations to national advertisers through an agency.
- Sell regional or national airtime for a radio network.
- Sell national air time for a syndicator of prepackaged radio programs.
- Sell air time for in-store radio programs.
- Sell air time for select programs on satellite radio.
- Sell program time or website advertising for internet radio stations.
- Sell radio programs to airlines for their in-flight entertainment packages.

Just by focusing, you have identified eight ways to accomplish your objective of "Radio Advertising Sales," all of which have a multitude of opportunities for you to explore.

What Do You Want?

See if you can tell what kind of jobs these people want from their objectives:

> "To obtain a position with a company that encourages the improvement of self and others, and demands a working professional code of ethics from all."

> "A career with a progressive organization that will utilize my education, skills, abilities and experience in an executive capacity, where I can effectively contribute to operations in any capacity that best matches my skills and experience."

> "An entry-level position in an organization that will utilize educational and work experience, eventually leading to supervisory and managerial functions."

> "Utilizing my experience and skills to develop a mutually beneficial work relationship and long-term affiliation with a reputable, stable and growth-oriented firm."

> "Seeking a position with an organization that follows a policy of recognition related to individual initiative and contribution. One that offers the opportunity to utilize a successful, creative and detail-oriented background to achieve the highest results."

> "To secure full-time employment with an integrated, international corporation, and through my diversified experience, aptitudes and skills, augment its effectiveness, motivate peers, and be instrumental and inventive in cost reduction while improving overall product and/or service delivery."

Here's my translation for all these objectives:

> "My objective is to get a job that pays well, allows me think and earn my money without working too hard, and won't disappear on me until and unless I'm ready to leave it."

But none of these objectives say the most important thing of all:

> "This is what I expect to be doing to earn my paycheck."

The last thing Mr. Bigg wants is an employee who is vague, indecisive, passive or noncommittal. But that's precisely the impression you make when you don't have a short, targeted objective on your resume.

Since Mr. Bigg can't guess what you want, don't make him figure it out. His gut reaction to a resume that doesn't have an objective is, "Why should I bother reading this?"

Reality Check

If you don't know what kind of job you want, don't expect someone else to decide for you. A targeted objective tells the Law of Attraction exactly what to bring into your life, and the clearer you are what that is, the more readily you will receive it.

If you have a vague or obscure objective, you are telling the Universe, "I don't care what kind of job I get," or "I want something in broadcasting" and you can count on receiving vague and obscure demonstrations of your hazy focus.

You will find the only kind of work you attract is as a checker at Wal-Mart or sweeping the TV studio as part of the janitorial staff. Since you were not specific, the Law of Attraction had nothing much to work with, so you got exactly what you asked for.

Imagine what would have happened instead if you had said, "I want to be a buyer of home accessories at a leading department store" or "I want to be in operations at a top television station in Chicago." Then as you pursued those positions, the Law of Attraction would make it easy for you to fulfill your vision.

How Can I Be Sure?

There is something you love to do – it fascinates you, you can't wait to do it, you lose sense of time while you're doing it, and you consider doing it a treat you give yourself.

It may be a hobby you've nurtured, a talent you never thought you could get paid to do or a passion you've promised yourself to explore someday.

Reality Check

There is almost always a way to combine what you know *how* to do with what you *love* to do and make a living at it.

For a few minutes, just go back to being a kid and indulge in some good, old-fashioned pretending when . . .

- You could do anything, be anyone and have everything you wanted.
- You were happy, loved, indulged, famous, talented, rich, popular and successful, if only in your imagination.
- You could create your own world that was just right for you, where no one could intrude and your every wish was granted.

Now, see yourself in your dream job. Where are you physically? Are you behind a desk in an office building or in an office at home? Are you in the field traveling on the way to a meeting with clients, in a boardroom doing a presentation, in the shop working with tools, or outdoors working with heavy equipment?

What kind of position do you have? Are you with groups of people or are you by yourself? What are you wearing – a suit, casual clothes, jeans or a uniform?

What sounds do you hear? What are you actually doing? What are you working on? Who is with you or are you alone? Most important of all, how do you feel being there and doing that?

Forget reality, forget job titles, forget companies, and forget industry trends. Forget the economy, forget the headlines and forget whether or not you think it's even possible. Just imagine you already have that job; doesn't it feel great?

Since you must first "be" before you can "have," don't be surprised if you end up in a job exactly like the one you imagined. After all, that's what you've been asking for!

Reality Check

The Universe doesn't know the difference between what you imagine to be real and what is real, so the Law of Attraction can be directed to turn your imagination into your reality. This is why your mind is the most powerful tool you have to bring your dream job – or anything else you desire – into your life.

Get to the Point

Once you have this vision of your dream job, write it down in precise detail so you can recreate the feeling that you already have it whenever you begin to doubt or lose focus.

Then boil down this detailed description to six words or less; this is your objective, which should be specific, but general enough to leave your options open, such as:

- Consumer Goods Marketing or Public Relations
- Investment Portfolio Research and Analysis
- Regional Bank Management
- Commercial Real Estate Appraisal and Analysis
- Employee Safety Coordination
- High School Administration
- Entertainment Law Paralegal
- Construction Engineering
- Software Programming and Development

Objectives Before and After

To effectively use my analytical skills in wastewater management to improve an employer's environmental operations.

Wastewater Analysis & Treatment

Accomplished administrator seeking to leverage an extensive background in personnel management, recruitment, employee relations

and benefits administration in an entry-level Human Resources position.
Corporate Human Resource Management/Administration

To apply the management-level supply chain and logistics skills gained during the last five years in a national retail organization to a director-level role in a consumer products organization.
Consumer Products Supply Chain/Logistics

A position in the health field using experience in organizing groups, clarifying ideas and problems, making public addresses and writing reports and newsletters.
Healthcare Marketing and Business Development

A position as an assistant to the curator of collections in a museum of art and/or natural history.
Assistant Curator

To obtain a meaningful and challenging position that enables me to learn the accounting field and allows for advancement.
Junior Accountant

To contribute strong technical skills and experience in a junior systems analyst capacity.
System Analyst

To obtain a position in manufacturing operations and development utilizing acquired knowledge and collective experience.
Manufacturing Operations and Development

Dynamic, award-winning career reflecting pioneering expertise in consultative sales and marketing of telecommunications network infrastructure equipment and services, seeking a position where the above skills and experience may be fully utilized and further developed.
Telecommunications Sales and Marketing

Debunked Resume Myth #6:
Job Descriptions Say It All

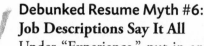

Under "Experience," put in any and all experiences that relate to, fulfill or support your objective. These could be class projects, freelance assignments, term papers, internships, work/study programs, volunteer work and, of course, paid jobs.

Reality Check

Your experiences should be no more than ten years old and be written to show how you, the group you worked with or the company you worked for, solved a problem.

The reason you only go back ten years has nothing to do with your age; it's because things have probably changed so much in your industry that anything past ten years is ancient history.

The Traditional System says to state your duties, responsibilities and achievements for each job in detail. After all, how else will Mr. Bigg know what you've done and can do for him?

Just for a moment, pretend you're Mr. Bigg. As you read the following Traditional System job descriptions, notice your feelings about these candidates from what they said about themselves:

A senior trainer at a large medical center described her job like this:

- Conduct approximately 15 days of training per month on a wide variety of management topics.
- Designed a one-day communication training program that received an organizational award.
- Consult with and/or coach approximately ten managers and supervisors monthly.
- Provide train-the-trainer sessions for 60 trainers annually.

A former real estate reporter for the Wall Street Journal wrote this about her job:

- Responsible for national real estate beat.
- Cover New York real estate and economic development.
- Write real estate column, news and feature stories.

- Work under daily deadlines.
- Generate story ideas.

A public relations director for the US division of an international commercial real estate company said this about her job:
- In charge of all press relations and advertising nationwide.
- Organize interviews between executives and journalists.
- Write and/or edit feature stories by our principals for inclusion in trade publications.
- Pitch stories to key editors of print and electronic media.
- Work closely with publications that sponsor roundtables and/or conferences.
- Devise PR/advertising strategies with executives to support new business efforts.

A technical editor described his job this way:
- Edited technical handbooks for a $170 million contract and coordinated the entire handbook production process.
- Oversaw writers and illustrators.
- Worked with computer-aided drawings.

A new graduate said this about an engineering internship:
- Assisted in experimental and literature research, prepared figures and data for technical papers and computed engineering calculations.

Another recent grad was an assistant instructor of rhetoric and composition, and described her internship like this:
- Evaluated an average of 75 student essays per semester, making comments intended to strengthen students' understanding of structure, argumentation, organization, coherence, flow, grammar and mechanics.
- Designed and delivered lectures, seminars and group exercises reinforcing these skills in an interactive, student-centered format using computer-based delivery methods.

Reality Check

Traditional System job descriptions are descriptions of jobs; they are lists of the tasks, functions and responsibilities that are expected and/or required of anyone who holds that position.

Salespeople sell, teachers teach, managers manage, accountants do accounting, computer programmers program computers, writers write; this is what people in those jobs are supposed to do, so no description of these functions is necessary.

A corporate trainer trains employees, develops training programs and consults with staff, managers and executives on issues that require training because corporate trainers are supposed to provide training to corporate employees.

A real estate reporter for a national newspaper has a national beat and generates columns, stories and features under deadline about real estate and economic development issues. Since she is a real estate reporter for a national newspaper, she is only doing what is expected of her.

An in-house public relations person handles press relations, arranges interviews, writes and edits company press material and supervises a company's promotional efforts. This is what an in-house PR person does for a living at any company, and anyone who hires her would expect her to do these things.

Technical editors edit technical handbooks, work with writers and illustrators, and know how to use a variety of computer drawing applications; that's why they're technical editors.

Interns are supposed to assist with whatever their superiors are working on, so it's no surprise an engineering intern would prepare figures and data for technical papers and compute engineering calculations. Grading papers and teaching classes are part of a teacher's job, so an assistant instructor is expected to assist with these things.

Reality Check

Mr. Bigg is not interested in what you did *on* your job; the only thing he wants to know is what you did *with* your job.

Because Mr. Bigg already has a pretty good idea of what you do or did just from your title, he doesn't care about your duties, responsibilities and achievements, so telling him all of this is a waste of his time and your energy.

Instead of giving a litany of your responsibilities or a lifeless listing of your achievements, first, put things in context by briefly describing the company you worked for, like this:

Big Boomer Company, New York (worldwide distributor of automobile accessories)

Chances are that Mr. Bigg won't know who your previous employers were, especially if you're from out of town, are changing industries, or have worked for small or unknown companies or for those that no longer exist.

Then, give one or two outstanding examples of a problem and how you, or the group you worked with or the company you worked for, solved that problem. For example:

◆ The trainer should have discussed some of the programs she developed and explained what they involved, why she needed to develop them and how they benefited the hospital.

◆ The reporter could have discussed some of the more interesting stories she covered, investigative reports she was involved with and the people and properties she wrote about.

◆ The engineering intern could have discussed the project he worked on – what it was for, how it worked and whether the program fulfilled its objectives.

◆ The assistant instructor might have discussed a challenging assignment or student, or what was different or unique about the curriculum she taught and/or helped develop.

Reality Check

To project yourself as a professional, downplay your individual role and describe the project and/or situation that your group, department or company was involved with.

Because you were part of the group or company, you can bask in its reflected glory, and you can legitimately share the credit for its achievements, regardless of what, how much or how little you actually did. This is called being a "team player."

Why Did You Do That?

As a boss, Mr. Bigg has a broad view of his department or company, and he will expect you to have one as well, so think about the following questions as you write your success stories:

- What was going on in your company at the time?
- What was the problem or situation?
- How did it affect your department, company or client?
- How was the situation addressed?
- Who else was involved in handling the situation?
- What happened as a result of what was done?

Here's what an accountant said about her job:

> "Managed three sets of books, worked directly with the Controller to oversee 12 divisions for a firm with annual revenues in excess of $125 million."

Accountants manage books and work directly with a controller to oversee a company's financial health. Since this is what accountants do during the normal part of their work, providing this information is redundant and unnecessary.

What this accountant failed to mention, but is of great interest to controllers at companies where she is applying, is that her employer had recently been acquired by an international conglomerate.

By taking a larger view of the situation and writing from Mr.

Bigg's perspective, this accountant's story is totally different, while being completely accurate and truthful:

> "Due to a takeover by an international conglomerate, the company restructured its operations from 17 divisions down to 12 in a period of six months, while maintaining annual revenues in excess of $125 million.

> "As part of the Corporate Finance team, my work included managing three sets of books while working with the Controller to ensure a smooth, seamless conversion to the new owners' reporting systems."

Before, this applicant was just crunching numbers like any accountant. But now, Mr. Bigg knows she can perform superbly under duress, while effectively handling difficult situations as part of a management team without losing her cool. And she never blew her own horn.

Here's what a distribution manager said about his work:

> "Designed an employee productivity improvement incentive program resulting in a 28% increase in productivity. Developed a seasonal staffing program eliminating the need for temporary labor, which resulted in a $500,000 savings."

The unanswered questions here are why the employee productivity improvement incentive program was needed in the first place and what the program entailed. It's a good bet that Mr. Bigg has similar productivity issues, and would be very interested in knowing more about this situation. Here's the fuller story:

> "Although our sales were up, profits were down, so senior management imposed a hiring freeze across the board. This hit distribution especially hard because our turnover is traditionally high due the seasonal nature of the work, resulting in a large demand for temporary labor.

"To address this situation, we developed a productivity improvement program exclusively for distribution. Our employees earned bonus pay, additional paid time off or tuition reimbursement, and they loved it.

"The result was productivity rose 28% in six months at a nominal cost, and we totally eliminated the need for temporary labor, saving the company more than $500,000 a year."

Modesty Becomes You

Unless you worked completely independently as a one-person operation, you can't take all the credit for what went right. Doing so will only backfire, especially if you're in management or want to be.

Reality Check

To showcase yourself as team player or supervisor, downplay your own importance in your success stories, and give the credit to other individuals, the group or the company. This will make Mr. Bigg think highly of you like nothing else.

Notice how the distribution manager shares the credit for the successful incentive program with his colleagues: "we developed," "our employees," "we totally eliminated."

By using "we" and "our" instead of "I" and "my," this manager intentionally minimizes his role, proving he is the kind of leader people want to follow, without needing to boast or brag to make himself look important.

One is the Loneliest Number

To jazz up your success stories, use numbers as much as possible to quantify things like dollars saved, sales made, goals met, reading scores raised, etc., but make sure you explain the numbers in the context of your stories.

Saying you "increased productivity 28% in six months" means nothing unless you explain what the situation was and how that end result was accomplished.

Dear Mom . . .

The key to writing a successful success story is to imagine you are writing a letter about your work to your mother who is not quite sure what you do for a living. You know Mom will want to know:

◆ What happened?
◆ Who else was involved?
◆ Why was it important that you did that?
◆ What happened when you did that?

Mom doesn't know your industry and will be confused by technical terms, industry shortcuts, acronyms or vague statements. She's not interested in the history of the situation and couldn't care less about the details, but she wants to get a feel for the problem, understand your role in it and learn how it all turned out.

Since you're merely telling her a story, you would never dream of boasting about yourself or using keywords, power phrases or action verbs in an attempt to impress her. If you wouldn't use any of these gimmicks when you write to Mom, don't use them when you write to someone else.

Just tell Mom (in writing) a few really interesting stories from work in your own words so she can brag about you in her own words.

Reality Check

Forget about buzz terms, action verbs, power phrases and keywords. Just use plain, simple, everyday, ordinary, conversational English. After all, that's what Mr. Bigg uses.

CHAPTER EIGHT

Extreme Resume Makeovers

"Whatever you are ready for is ready for you."

– Mark Victor Hansen, Author

LET IT BE

"There is nothing good or bad, but thinking makes it so."

– William Shakespeare

Debunked Resume Myth #7:
Dates Are Really Important
In the Traditional System, dates are so important that there's a whole style of resume built around them – it's called the chronological resume.

Reality Check
The sole function of the chronological resume is to show when you did something. But it is not important when you did something, only that you did something.

The whole point of dates on a resume is they put you at certain places at a certain points in time so you can talk about what it was like being there then. Otherwise, dates are totally irrelevant.

In 1977, I was Operations Assistant at WABC-AM in New York City, the number one radio station in America. WABC played Top 40 pop music, had been number one for over a decade, and was legendary in the radio business for its ratings, its reputation and how it turned air time into tons of money.

I can talk about WABC during the waning days of Top 40 radio in New York because I was there then. I'm not there now, the music died at WABC in 1982, and the teen-oriented, Top 40 pop music format doesn't even exist anymore.

Now You See It, Now You Don't

Have you put your dates:

- All the way over on one side of the page so they form a column?
- Right up there with the name of the companies you used to work for so they're the first thing seen?
- On the bottom of the page as in a functional format so they're the last thing seen?
- Somewhere else on the page, but surrounded them with a lot of white space and/or bolded and/or italicized them so that they stand out?

If you have done any of these things, you have drawn attention to your dates. You have made your dates important! You are practically begging Mr. Bigg to look at your dates, and then when he looks at your dates, you complain that he's looking at your dates . . . but you asked him to!

Reality Check

To make your dates unobtrusive, put them in parentheses – years only – at the end of the last success story for each employer. When you put your dates like this, you will put the focus on *what* you did, not *when* you did it.

In the "Before and After" examples and in both of my resumes that follow, notice how all of the dates are there, but they are virtually invisible. You really have to hunt for them.

Resume One – Before

Objective: Experienced professional seeking a career position in the real estate field. Excellent organizational skills with ability to manage multiple properties for site acquisition, in addition to reviewing comprehensive legal data.

Relevant Work Experience

Denny's/El Polo Loco, Inc., Irvine, CA 2004 - 2006
Manager, Real Estate Acquisition

- Performed and managed 30 property acquisitions including legal review for California, Arizona and Florida.
- Coordinated surveys, soil tests and site plans to meet schedules for commencement of construction.
- Managed and coordinated real estate documents and closings for three-state area.
- Prepared and reviewed Non-Disturbance and Estoppel Agreements for leased properties.
- Managed lease data for 190 stores.

Kentucky Fried Chicken, Inc., Irving, TX 2002 - 2003
Real Estate Consultant

- Formulated demographic studies of 12 sites and presented comparative analysis.
- Collected and analyzed trade generators to determine quality of sites.
- Developed data analysis for D/FW county areas of all competitors for home delivery.
- Research data with local cities for each site.

Jiffy Lube Franchise, Dallas, TX 2000 - 2002
Director of Real Estate

- Negotiated real estate contractual terms and conditions up to $1 million.
- Coordinated zoning changes through local city councils.
- Managed all real estate transactions from site selection through legal closings.

Brown & Shapiro Law Firm, Dallas, TX 1999 - 2001
Office Manager
- ◆ Organized and managed new branch office for preparation of real estate documents.
- ◆ Processed over 100 closings a month.
- ◆ Supervised and trained personnel for data review.

Hamilton/Owen Real Estate, Garland, TX 1993 - 1999
Real Estate Sales Representative
- ◆ 1996 Realtor of the Year Bernays award
- ◆ Multi-million dollar producer
- ◆ Top salesperson, summer 1995
- ◆ Guest speaker for local, state and national Realtor groups.

Pizza Inn, Inc., Dallas, TX 1990 – 1993
Contract Administrator
- ◆ Organized efficient lease data system, saving the company thousands of dollars for over 150 company stores.
- ◆ Reviewed and managed all property purchase transactions.

Education
University of Oklahoma, Norman, OK 1988 – 1990
- ◆ Paralegal Certificate
- ◆ Business/Psychology major. 70 credit hours.
- ◆ Currently working on a degree in Business Management which includes 12 hours law.

Professional Accomplishments
- ◆ Listed in Who's Who of American Women, 2001- 2002 and 2003 - 2004
- ◆ Dallas Realtor of the Year Bernay's Award 1996

Associations
- ◆ Member, Commercial Real Estate Women
- ◆ Former member, credit review committee of Women's Federal Credit Union

Resume One – After

OBJECTIVE: Retail Site Selection

Experience

As Manager, Real Estate Administration, for Denny's/El Pollo Loco, Inc. (Irvine, CA), I spearheaded the selection, acquisition and administration of 200 free-standing restaurant pad sites along major thoroughfares and in shopping centers in Arizona, California and Florida.

Some of these sites posed legal, environmental and/or financial challenges, and our team worked hand-in-hand with local organizations and funding sources to ensure a smooth transition of ownership.

One large site had been planned for a motel/restaurant development. However, wetlands at the edge of the property delayed construction until an environmental impact analysis was conducted and remediation plans had been approved by the state's environmental commission. The project was built and is a huge success. (2004 – 2006)

Previously, I was a real estate consultant for Kentucky Fried Chicken, Inc. (Irving, TX), where I worked with a team of analysts providing market research critical to the selection and acquisition of 30 potential free-standing restaurant sites within the Dallas Metroplex.

As part of this work, I conducted an in-depth analysis of KFC's competition, which provided a demographic picture of restaurant locations within the Metroplex. Kentucky Fried Chicken used this study to establish its new home delivery service, which exceeded all its initial expectations. (2002 – 2003)

While Director of Real Estate for a franchise of Jiffy Lube. Inc., (Dallas, TX), I coordinated the selection, acquisition and approval of more than a dozen sites within the metropolitan area.

The major issue for Jiffy Lube was environmental; the cities in which the sites were located were concerned that run-off from these sites would pollute the local ground water supplies, and initially refused to approve the needed zoning changes.

To address this issue, I gave a series of presentations to the zoning commissions, local chambers of commerce and other community groups on the precautions Jiffy Lube takes to prevent hazardous spills and how the company is environmentally friendly. The zoning changes were subsequently approved. (2000-2002)

Education
University of Oklahoma, Certificate in Paralegal Studies (2000)

Various courses and seminars in real estate marketing, finance, law and real estate investment at the University of Texas at Arlington and Southern Methodist University. Texas Real Estate Salesperson's license currently being renewed.

Other Information
- Realtor of the Year (1996 recipient of the Lois Hair Bernays Cup)
- Greater Dallas Board of Realtors
- Participant in the planning of the National Association of Realtors' 1996 conference
- Who's Who of American Woman in 2001-2002 and 2003 – 2004
- Member, Commercial Real Estate Women, Dallas

Resume Two — Before

Exploration/Development geophysicist with 20 oil and 8 gas field career discoveries and 66 successful development wells. Seek to continue success with an exploration/ exploitation company.

EXPERIENCE

Senior Staff Geophysicist, Nearburg Producing Company - Dallas, TX 1991-Feb 2006

As the sole company geophysicist, I was responsible for all exploration/development geophysics in the Gulf Coast and Permian Basin. Main duty was integrated regional mapping and prospect generation with 3 exploration geologists as well as evaluation of industry proposals.

- Responsible for seismic budget, acquisition, processing, data management, integrated interpretation, economic analysis and presentation to management.
- Full seismic involvement, from 3D design through interpretation and reservoir characterization, to locate dolomite porosity and pick the locations for 57 producers in a Pennsylvanian carbonate play in Eddy County, NM.
- Generated prospects and picked the locations for ten Pennsylvanian algal mound producers in Lea County, NM.
- Generated the prospect and locations for a three-well field in southeast New Mexico.
- Applied AVO techniques to gas sand exploration in the Gulf Coast and Permian Basin.
- Integrated mapping and picked locations for 18 Morrow prospects - results 11 gas wells.
- Seismic evaluation of 48 geologic leads in Midland Basin. Recommended drilling six prospects resulting in two gas wells and one oil well.
- Nine years Seismic MicroTechnology Kingdom workstation experience.
- Use Petra, I.H.S., DrillingInfo.com and Rose risk analysis software.

Geophysical Consultant – Littleton, CO 1986-1991

- Generated prospect and picked locations for a ten-well field in Gaines County, Texas.
- Seismic evaluation and picked locations for seven successful field discoveries as the consultant for six clients involved in SE New Mexico and W. Texas exploration plays.

Professional Geophysicist, Amerada Hess Corporation - Denver, CO 1984-1986
As sole geophysicist in an exploration team, I completed interpretation of 420 miles of 2D and a 3D seismic survey for three mapping horizons.

- Picked drill site for five producers in SE New Mexico.
- Forecast drill results on farmout acreage with 80% accuracy, as a result, leases were evaluated at no cost to the company.
- Coordinated seismic activity, leasing and drill site locations for Britoil and Inexco Oil Companies.

Geophysicist, Getty Oil Company – Midland, TX 1979-1984

- Interpreted seismic activity, recommended lease acquisition and picked drill sites for a four-well oil field discovery in the northern Midland Basin.
- Generated oil and gas prospects in the Fort Worth Basin, Eastern Shelf and northern Midland Basin.
- Mentored two geophysics graduates in seismic interpretation.
- Originated, organized and interpreted an induced polarization electrical survey to evaluate 21 prospects throughout the Permian Basin.

Geophysicist, Seismograph Service Corporation – Tulsa, OK 1972-1979

- Interpreted data for client exploration in the Anadarko and Illinois Basins U.S.A., as well as a 1,000+ mile 2D program in the Gulf of Kutch, India.
- Identified potential gas storage structures from Appalachian Basin 2D seismic.
- Generated interpretation and reports for numerous clients in the search for Silurian Niagaran reefs and exploitation along the Albion-Scipio trench in Michigan.

EDUCATION

- B.S. Geology, 1970, University of Missouri - Rolla
- PETRA training
- IHRDC-Economic Evaluation of Petroleum Projects

- AAPG Collage Tectonics
- Getty sponsored courses in effective writing, economic evaluation, acoustic impedance logs, basic management and seismic stratigraphy.

SEG, AAPG, Dallas Geophysical Society and Permian Basin Geophysical Society, Texas Geoscientist #1234.

....

Resume Two – After

OBJECTIVE: Oil/Gas Exploration/Development Geophysics

Experience
Nearburg Producing Company, Dallas, TX (privately-held oil and gas producer in the Permian Basin and Gulf Coast)

As the sole geophysicist, my work encompassed all areas of exploration and development for the company's operations, particularly using seismic inversion techniques and applied attention to detail. This approach has resulted in numerous successful finds with a minimum of dry wells:

- Nearburg had a 4,000-acre leasehold interest near Carlsbad, NM that preliminary research had indicated would contain significant finds. Over a three-year period, we drilled 56 productive wells out of 60 wells drilled, averaging 400 cum MBO per well.

- In a New Mexico site near Hobbs, we drilled 24 wells, 16 of which were productive, averaging 240 cum MBO per well.
- In Midland where 48 geographic leads were located, I recommended drilling six prospective wells. Three were productive: two gas wells and one oil well. (1991-2006)

Independent Geophysical Consultant, Littleton, CO
As a consultant specializing in oil and gas exploration and development, I worked with such companies as:

Branex Petroleum, Roswell, NM
Columbia Oil & Gas, Denver
Heyco, Roswell, NM
Nearburg Producing Company, Dallas
Yates Petroleum, Artesia, NM

For these and other companies, I picked locations that resulted in productive wells. One client leased a site in Gaines County, TX, and under my guidance, they drilled ten wells, all of which produced with a EUR of 4 MM BOE. (1986-1991)

Other Information
Texas Registered Geoscientist; Member, Society of Exploration Geophysicists; Member, American Association of Petroleum Geologists; Member, Dallas Geophysical Society; Member, Permian Basin Geophysical Society.

Education
University of Missouri – Rolla, B.S. Geology, 1970

....

Resume Three – Before

Objective: To contribute media buying savvy and skills in a permanent position as a spot broadcast media buyer.

Experience
Broadcast Media Coordinator, S.R. Oakley & Company, Tampa, FL August 2004 - Present

- Negotiate and place spot broadcast media buys in two markets.
- Assist Senior Broadcast Negotiator on maintenance of all buys in four additional markets.
- Process market revisions.
- Coordinate added value opportunities.
- Order media buys and check against contracts.
- Evaluate make-goods and resolve discrepancies.
- Conduct quarterly post-buy analysis.
- Provide planning with market conditions and projected cost per points.

Intern, PepsiCo Bottling, Orlando, FL May - July 2003
- Researched and reported on sampling in five markets in Florida and South Georgia.
- Monitored local store displays.
- Attended Orlando market radio review.
- Collected air checks from radio promotions involving Pepsi products.

Internet Researcher, Dr. Randall Hansen, Associate Professor of Marketing, Stetson University, Deland, FL August 2002 - May 2002
- Searched internet for writing-related websites to be included in Dr. Hansen's book, Write Your Way to a Higher GPA
- Created links to writing-related internet sites for the book's related writing and editing resources website.

Education
- Bachelor of Business Administration, Stetson University, Deland, Florida, 2004, Major: Marketing
- Honors: Marketing Assistant of the Year Award, 2003
- Computer Skills
- Knowledge of Reflections (Datatrak) buying software
- Microsoft Office Experience in HTML web design

Resume Three – After

Objective: Broadcast Media Buyer

Experience

As a Broadcast Media Coordinator for S.R. Oakley & Company (Tampa), I am part of the team that develops media buys, programs and packages for a ream of clients.

One of our clients asked us to coordinate an extensive package of radio, television, internet and in-store media buys. Our team worked in tandem with his advertising agency, which handled the print media, and his public relations agency, which handled the product promotion, sampling and testing.

This project took three months to plan, six months to execute and three months to evaluate. The product was a huge success, and sales of the line continue to exceed projections. (2004 – Present)

Being a Pepsi lover, doing an internship at PepsiCo Bottling in Orlando was a dream come true. I learned from the inside how soft drinks and related products are developed, tested and introduced locally before they are marketed nationally.

While I was there, PepsiCo was testing a low-calorie, sparkling cranberry juice to appeal to dieters, those wanting an alternative to soda, and more sophisticated buyers of nonalcoholic beverages.

As part of the promotional team, I set up store displays, monitored air checks from local radio stations and handed out samples to consumers. (2003)

Education

MBA in marketing, University of Florida, in progress
Stetson University, Deland, Florida , B.A. Marketing, 2004

Other Information
Member, American Marketing Association
Member, Association of Women in Communications
National Association of Minority Media Executives

....

Janet's Resume As A Young Professional

Objective: Commercial Real Estate Public Relations/Marketing

Experience
As Manager of Real Estate Development Services for Energy & Environmental Analysts, Inc. (Garden City, NY), I conceived and administered a marketing program to provide developers with environmental consulting services. This included writing "New York City's Environmental Review Process for Real Estate – A Guide for Developers."

I also edited the firm's environmental impact statements, and wrote its land use and socio-economic sections. (1982 – 1984)

While a consultant to Queens Community Board #6 (Forest Hills, NY), I analyzed the potential economic impacts a proposed regional mall would have on the surrounding neighborhoods.

I presented my findings to the New York City Planning Commission in oral testimony at its public hearing on the mall, and my analysis was incorporated into the Community Board's recommendation to the city's Board of Estimate. Much to the relief of the community, the mall was never built. (1980 - 1982)

As a staff member of Mall Properties, Inc., I was involved in all phases of the firm's development activities – from project conception, land assemblage, financing and regulatory approvals, through construction, leasing and management.
I assisted in the development and preleasing of a regional mall in

Connecticut with major environmental issues, and the marketing of a subdivision in Pennsylvania. (1978 - 1980)

Education
New York University, Masters of Urban Planning, 1982
New York University Real Estate Institute, Certificate in Real Estate Studies, 1982
Adelphi University, B.A., 1974

Other information
Member, Real Estate Board of New York; Member, Association of Real Estate Women (New York); New York State Real Estate Salesperson

As a commercial real estate writer, I've been published in Real Estate Forum, Real Estate Weekly, National Mall Monitor, Better Buildings and Newsday. My industry analyses include "Reflections on a Regional Mall: The Forest Hills Galleria (1982), "Doing Business in Dutch Kills" (1981) and "Shopping in the City: An Urban Mall Experience" (1981).

....

Janet's Current Resume

Objective: Durable Medical Equipment Sales

Experience
I'm currently president of Bariatrics Unlimited, LLC, (Plano, TX), which sells patient care equipment for the obese (300 lbs. +) to hospitals and nursing homes nationwide. Since one-third of Americans are either obese or overweight, this niche market is just beginning to show its true potential.

One new hospital in Oklahoma was positioning itself as a "no-lift" facility to ensure the safety of its nurses and patients. Because it was specializing in weight loss surgeries, the hospital wanted three power gurneys, but the ones available from a major manufacturer weren't wide enough.

Working with my manufacturer of power wheelchairs and stretchers for quadriplegics, we were able to build and deliver three custom-made power gurneys to the hospital in time for the opening of its bariatric wing. (2001 – Present)

Previously, I was the rehab sales representative in Texas and Oklahoma for Otto Bock Health Care (Minneapolis, MN). My role was to educate rehab dealers and therapists at facilities on the company's unique seating and positioning products, bath equipment and mobility products. (2000 - 2001)

As an outside sales rep for Amigo Mobility Center (Grand Prairie, TX), I generated scooter sales and rehab referrals, and brought in seven new PPO and HMO insurance contracts.

In one year, I spoke to more than 130 senior centers and groups, senior health centers, disabled groups, home health agencies, assisted and independent living facilities around the Metroplex. (1998 - 2000)

Prior to joining Amigo, I helped build Scooters To Go, Inc. (Dallas) from a two-person start-up to a major local provider of scooters and power wheelchairs. (1996 – 1998)

Before getting into healthcare, I spent 12 years as a commercial real estate publicist and freelance trade writer. For nine of those 12 years, I ran my own agency, White Marketing Services, and served national and regional commercial real estate companies in New York and Dallas. (1984 - 1996)

Education
Basic seminars and programs in rehab seating and positioning given by Crown Therapeutics, Graham-Field, Invacare, Pride Healthcare and Sunrise Medical (1996 – 1999)

New York University, Masters in Urban Planning, 1982
Adelphi University, BA, 1974

....

Excuse Me, Your Age Is Showing
The Traditional System believes that if you are over 40, you:

◆   Face exceptionally difficult challenges in getting hired.

◆   Must resort to resume illusions, cosmetic makeovers and ward-
    robe overhauls to disguise your real age.

◆   Have stopped learning or growing, are functionally obsolete,
    and are incapable of contributing anything of substance to the
    workforce or the world.

◆   Lack ambition, are unable or unwilling to try or learn anything
    new, and can only be hired for jobs no one else wants.

One website says:

> "If you are over 40 and scouting the job market, be prepared
> to compete with younger applicants who represent a bundle of
> energy and enthusiasm, are willing to work for less pay, and are
> generally more savvy concerning the latest technology."

And if you're over 50, Monster.com has some advice for you:

> "There are instances where your age will interfere with your can-
> didacy and no matter what you do, that will not change. If you
> know you're fighting an uphill battle, retreat and forget it."

This "advice" buys into the Traditional System belief that older candidates and younger candidates are competing for the same job and,
other than age, are relatively comparable.

The fact is, once Mr. Bigg talks to you and certainly once he meets you, he'll know you're not 38, 48 or even 58. Whatever age you are, that is what you are, and by trying to hide your age, you only draw attention to it.

Reality Check

Your age is irrelevant; what matters is what you know, have done, have learned and can apply on the job to help Mr. Bigg with what he needs. Unless you are in show business, you simply cannot be 30 years old and have 20 years experience.

You should be proud of your age instead of trying to hide it. Your years on this planet give you an edge your younger associates can't begin to match because you know things that come only with time, training and experience – none of which your junior counterparts have. If they're lucky, one day they might be as old as you are and know half what you do.

So you think you're "too old" to get hired? Oh, really? Are you are too old to: Think? Make decisions? Be creative? Do your thing? Be happy in your work? Be fairly compensated? Since when does the number of birthdays you've had count against you?

Reality Check

Like everything else, your belief about your age becomes your experience. When you stop believing your age is a problem in your getting hired, it will cease to be one.

Robert Mitchell of Dallas refused to let his age be a limitation to achieving his dream. At the age of 52, he decided to become a Religious Science minister, but lacked the bachelor's degree required for ministerial school.

So Robert rearranged his life and found a distance-learning college that fed his spirit as well as his mind. Simultaneously, he began a rigorous, three-year course of study to become a Religious Science licensed practitioner (a designation required for ministerial school); he also was working full time.

Three years later, at age 55, Robert had both his college degree and practitioner designation, and now was qualified to begin another three years of study as a ministerial student.

Upon graduation from ministerial school at age 58, Robert still wasn't done. In Religious Science, new ministers must complete a two-year term of service before they can be ordained.

So, Robert worked as assistant minister at the Center for Spiritual Living in Dallas for two years, and even though he was finished with his formal training, he was still taking extra classes to specialize as a counselor.

Finally, at age 60, eight years after he set his goal, Rev. Robert Mitchell was ordained as a Religious Science minister at the Center for Spiritual Living.

And how did he feel about finally reaching his goal after such a long time, when so many people his age are thinking of slowing down? At his ordination party, Rev. Robert remarked, "My life has just begun."

Debunked Resume Myth #8
The Little Stuff Matters
No, it doesn't. The rest is just semi-important filler.

Education
In this section, you put college or trade school information, and any graduate degrees and/or professional training programs you have completed, like this: "Dallas University, B.A. 1975."

You can put in your major, but only if it relates to your objective, and only if you have been out of college for a year or less. Once you're out of college, everything related to your undergraduate experience is irrelevant, unless it relates to your objective.

The fact is that most people end up doing something totally different from what they majored in; this is called "life." You do not have to work at something that no longer suits you or you don't like just because you took a few courses in it in college.

It is perfectly fine for you to change your mind about what you'd like to do for a living two, ten, 20 or 40 years down the road. You need no one's approval or permission to change your mind and change your life, except your own.

If you attended but didn't finish college, put the name of the school and the years you attended. If you are completing college, graduate school or a training program, put it down like this: "New York University, MBA in Finance, in progress."

Do not list your courses because it will be assumed you took courses that are relevant to your degree and if you didn't, why would you mention them? Do not put your anticipated completion date because life happens.

Include any nondegree professional courses leading to a certificate or designation related to your objective you have taken, but only if they are within the last five years because anything before then will indicate your training is out of date.

Basic courses in computers, business or your industry don't count, nor do continuing education seminars in your profession which are required for a license or designation. You don't get brownie points for doing what you're supposed to be doing anyway.

Other Information
Here you put all your objective-relevant memberships in business, trade or civic organizations; activities or leadership roles held; awards, honors or outstanding achievements; qualifying licenses not listed under Education, and so on.

Personal Information
Your resume is not an autobiographic work history, so your age, height, weight, marital status, name of your spouse, ages of your children and your hobbies should never be on it. Besides, have you ever seen a resume that says, "Health: Poor to Lousy"?

Layout
Your resume is an introduction to you, and good introductions are short. Keep your resume to one page if at all possible, the paragraphs to five lines maximum, and double space between paragraphs.

Capitalize proper nouns, names and places; use centering, italics, and bolding or underlining (other than headings) sparingly; and don't overdo it with fancy graphics.

Keep your resume neat and clean with at least one-inch margins and lots of white space so that it's easy to read. Mr. Bigg's very human eyes have a natural tendency to bounce, and short paragraphs and lots of white space allow them to relax and go wherever they want on the page without effort or strain.

When you have a page crammed with information, Mr. Bigg will intuitively resist what he is reading – and you – and won't know why.

Use any writing style, layout and font you are comfortable with – this is *your* resume, after all.

Reality Check

If you write your resume from Mr. Bigg's perspective in language your mother can understand, you simply cannot write a bad resume.

CHAPTER NINE

Covers Letters Revealed

*"I'll bet a few well-placed pieces of correspondence,
and I get to be a queen in no time."*

*– Lucy van Pelt in
"You're a Good Man, Charlie Brown"*

STARING AT THAT BLANK PAGE

"What do you say to a guy in a letter, anyway?"

– Rizzo in Grease

ow you've come to the hard part – you actually have to contact the person you want to work for. Unless you're very good at talking with total strangers on the phone, you'll have to do this by email or regular mail.

Email

Sure, it's easy (if you know their email address), fast and cheap, but conducting a job search by email has tremendous pitfalls. It's a good bet that you delete junk emails and won't open emails with attachments from people you don't know.

Well, like it or not, Mr. Bigg does exactly the same thing. And that's assuming your email even makes it to his in-box; thanks to sophisticated spam filters, he may never even see it.

Reality Check

The best way to use email is after you have spoken to Mr. Bigg. That way, he'll be expecting your email, will open it and read it.

And don't think you can trick Mr. Bigg into opening your email by using a snazzy subject line. This gimmick may work once, but you'll come across as amateurish and insincere, and destroy any chance you might have had of getting hired.

Regular (Snail) Mail

When email first hit the business world, it was new, exciting and cutting-edge. But now that email is commonplace, regular mail is the preferred method for sending a cold call letter, simply because a snail mail letter exists in the physical world.

Mr. Bigg has to hold your letter while he's reading it and then do something with it: file it away, put it on a pile, give it to someone else or throw it out. But it just may float on his desk for a time, something that can't happen with your email unless he prints it out, which is unlikely.

Brrr! That's A Cold Call Letter

In the Traditional System, your killer cover letter is written to decimate your competition and prove why you are the only possible choice for the job.

Your "knock 'em dead" letter is supposed to entice Mr. Bigg into calling you by providing an in-depth description of where you've worked, what you've done and what phenomenal personal and professional qualities you have that no one else on the planet (including him) possesses.

Confident you'll soon be offered an interview, you send off your letter and wait. But there is no call, no email, no response at all. Eventually, you realize Mr. Bigg isn't getting back to you. What happened? Why doesn't he want to see you?

Reality Check

Your Traditional System cover letter fails to impress Mr. Bigg because it is all about you. There isn't a word in it about Mr. Bigg – what he wants, what he's interested in or how he will benefit from knowing you. In other words, the reason Mr. Bigg doesn't want to see you is because there's no reason to.

The next time you get some junk mail or spam email, notice how the writers attempt to get you to do what they want by telling you about themselves or what they want you to buy, and especially notice how you feel about them. Well, that's just how Mr. Bigg feels about you when you write a Traditional System cover letter that is all about you.

A Traditional Cover Letter

Here is the structure of a typical Traditional System cover letter:

First Paragraph: Why You're Writing

You introduce yourself, specify the kind of job you want and outline what you can offer. Because employers will make quick judgments, a good opening line is essential. Mention how you heard about the job and/or what you know about the company.

Second Paragraph: Why They Should Hire You

Describe the contributions you can make and what qualifications, experiences, or personal qualities you posses that would make you a valuable employee. List your qualifications by using specific examples of your achievements to avoid vague generalities about your experiences or qualifications.

Third Paragraph: Call to Action

The closing paragraph must propel the potential employer to take action with respect to your application. Note that you are enclosing a resume and express your desire to meet in the near future the person to whom you are writing. Close the letter by thanking them for their consideration in order to express gratitude for taking time to read your letter.

Reality Check

The problem with a Traditional System cover letter is that it's a pitch piece about you. But unless you're a batter in a baseball game, no one, including Mr. Bigg, likes to be pitched.

Webster's definitions of pitch includes: "to throw, usually with a particular objective or toward a particular point; to sell or advertise, especially in a high pressure way; to utter glibly and insincerely."

So, when you write a Traditional System cover letter, you are glibly and insincerely using high-pressure sales tactics to throw yourself at Mr. Bigg without the slightest regard for his regard. Is *this* the impression you really want to make?

A Contrarian Cover Letter

A Contrarian System cover letter doesn't pitch, make your case, or sell you in any way; instead, it helps Mr. Bigg buy you.

Reality Check

Don't write to Mr. Bigg about what's important to you; write about what's important to him. And how do you know what's important to him? From all that research you did in the beginning!

Here is the structure of a Contrarian System cover letter:

First to Second Paragraph: The Grabber

This opening is designed to catch Mr. Bigg's attention, draw him into the body of the letter, and make him want to keep reading. Ideally, it should:

- Contain a referral ("John Jones at ABC Corporation suggested I contact you about your . . .")
- Recap a function you both attended ("It was a pleasure meeting you last week at the meeting of . . .") or
- Summarize his comments if he was the speaker at a function ("Thank you for speaking to our group last week about your new approach to . . .").

Use these openings if you have them, but chances are that you will have none of them. Instead, make a general comment about an industry trend, news about the company, the company's latest venture, a change you've noticed in their packaging, an event it's involved with – something, anything Mr. Bigg can relate to.

If you do your homework about the company you want to work for and its products and/or services, how it stacks up against its competition, what it is involved with and what is happening in the world affecting it, you can easily find something to write about.

Second to Third Paragraph: Identify Mr. Bigg's Problem

Now suggest – not tell – Mr. Bigg that he may be faced with a problem or an area of opportunity, and then briefly discuss this problem or area of opportunity without offering solutions.

Contrary to what the Traditional System teaches, one of the worst things you can do when you're job hunting is to offer Mr. Bigg solutions as an incentive for him to want to meet you. (See "Tell You What I'm Gonna Do" below.)

Reality Check

If you offer solutions, claim to be the answer to Mr. Bigg's problem, or give examples of how you solved similar problems, Mr. Bigg will know you are trying to sell him, and you will destroy any credibility he has given you up to this point.

But when you discuss an issue Mr. Bigg may be facing without offering solutions, he will automatically credit you with having insight into his problem or opportunity, and will assume you have some ideas on how to help him.

Third to Fourth Paragraph: Maybe I Can Help

By this time, Mr. Bigg is feeling very good about you, and he naturally wants to know something about you. Only now do you briefly mention who you are and how there's a possibility you might be able to help him.

This should intentionally be written as an aside with the tone of, "Oh, by the way, here's some information on me, but it's really not too important."

Reality Check
If you want Mr. Bigg to want to know more about you, say as little as possible about yourself, downplay your own importance and keep your letter focused on him, his company and his situation.

Never use the word "resume" in your letter because it tells Mr. Bigg you want a job, rather than wanting to help him. To keep Mr. Bigg from instinctively tuning you out, use "information," "background," or "material" instead of "resume."

Fourth to Fifth Paragraph: Never Can Say Goodbye
Most Traditional System cover letters end limply, implying that you are no longer responsible for getting yourself hired and it's all up to Mr. Bigg now:

◆ "Thank you for your consideration."
◆ "I look forward to hearing from you."
◆ "I would appreciate any assistance you can give me."

When you use these phrases, you may think you're being polite, but actually, you come across as being weak, passive, ineffective and wimpy.

Reality Check
When you take responsibility for follow-up, it proves you are capable and reliable, can take the initiative, see a project through and get things done – without your having to say it.

The best way to end your letter is to cordially tell Mr. Bigg you will be calling him in a week and then thank him for his time. After all, if everything goes right, you're going to be taking up a great deal more of it very soon.

The "I versus You" Test
Here is a very easy way to know if you have written an effective cover letter and what to do about it if you haven't:

- Count the number of "I's" – "I," "me," "my," "us," "our," and/or "we" referring to yourself, your current company or your previous employers.

- Count the number of "you's" – "you," "your," Mr. Bigg's name, the name of his company and/or other people you know or have talked to in his company.

- The use of "we," "us" and "our" when referring to yourself and Mr. Bigg cancel each other out and are not counted.

- If there are more I's than you's, or if your letter is clearly about you even if it has more you's than I's, rip it up and start all over. You've written about the wrong person.

The "It's Really About Me" Trap

Don't try to justify why you should be hired by making your letter sound like it's about Mr. Bigg when it's really about you. He'll know exactly what you're doing, and you'll only be fooling yourself, like in these examples:

Here's Why You Should Hire Me

As marketing companies are increasingly called upon to supply information on magazine readership to publishers, there is a growing need for trained, experienced professionals in the field.

Through my marketing research experiences and my master's thesis, which have particularly dealt with improving marketing research studies so they can better define magazine audiences to potential advertisers, I am certain I could give you valuable assistance in satisfying research demands, managing key projects, and improving the marketing tools you currently use.

I will be completing my master's degree in December, and would be interested in making a significant contribution to the Research Institute's profitability in a marketing research capacity. I am sure my services would be useful to you, and I will call you in early October to discuss an interview.

Score: I's: 9 You's: 5

Comments: The first part of the grabber is fine because it is about an issue Mr. Bigg is most likely dealing with. But the second part makes it clear that the rest of the letter is going to be a rationalization about why the applicant should be hired.

The applicant then attempts to prove she is an ideal researcher, yet she never once mentions anything about the Research Institute, what it does, what it's involved with or what some of its particular challenges or opportunities might be.

Here's what Mr. Bigg thinks of her: how good of a researcher can she be when she can't even do basic research about the research firm she want to do research for?

How Could You Not Want Me?

From our conversation, it sounds as if you're looking for someone to come in and take charge immediately. It also sounds like you are experiencing problems with some of your database systems.

With my seven years of experience working with financial databases, I've saved companies thousands of dollars by streamlining systems. My high energy and quick learning style enable me to hit the ground and size up problems rapidly.

My colleagues would tell you I'm a team player who maintains a positive attitude and outlook. I have the ability to stay focused in stressful situations and can be counted on when the going gets tough. I'm confident I would be a great addition to your team.

Score: I's: 9 You's: 5

Comments: This letter started off fine; obviously, the two of them had talked about Mr. Bigg's issues with his database, so the applicant knew the specific problems the company has and how important it was to get the database fixed quickly.

His letter should have recapped their conversation, but instead, this job seeker chose to brag about how wonderful he thought he was. Not surprisingly, Mr. Bigg found someone more interested in fixing his database than in making himself look good.

Whose Letter Is This, Anyway?

Each of the following Traditional System cover letters is scored with comments following and then rewritten as a Contrarian System letter from Mr. Bigg's perspective:

Letter #1: Are You Impressed Yet?

I am extremely interested in exploring advancement opportunities of employment with Juarez Foods. After a brief perusal of my resume, you will agree that my experience, training and education make me a strong candidate for a sales position at Juarez Foods.

With my more than 25 years of sales management, financial administration, account representation, customer service management, and marketing experience, I would be an instant asset to your organization.

I have a proven track record of high achievement with each of my sales positions, being quickly assigned additional responsibilities and receiving promotions due to my continual outstanding performances.

I possess exceptional people skills, thrive on resolving challenges, and prefer employment within a sales and marketing team environment. I am detail oriented, easily set and accomplish goals, and specialize in multi-tasking while keeping my focus on the big picture.

One of my strongest assets is developing relationships with my customers to promote a win-win environment. Please allow me the opportunity to interview as soon as possible.

I can assure you that if I am offered the Sales Associate position at Juarez Foods, it will be one of the soundest hiring decisions you could ever make. I look forward to hearing from you soon.

Score: I's: 18 You's: 8

Comments: A typical Traditional System cover letter, this letter pounds away at Mr. Bigg in order to impress him. Mr. Bigg is impressed all right – all that buffoonery and self-importance has given him a headache.

Did you notice the ending – how this take-charge, hard-hitting, aggressive salesman becomes meek and subservient, and then humbly awaits Mr. Bigg's call?

By abdicating responsibility for follow-up, this applicant proves his claims about his ability to sell were just hype, and he comes across as a passive paper-pusher who prefers taking orders from established accounts rather than going out and finding new ones.

Here is the same letter written from the Sales Director's point of view:

Letter #1 Rewrite: Facing the Challenge

In a recent article in Supermarket News, you said large supermarkets are resistant to carrying local ethnic brands, despite their popularity with consumers, especially in urban markets.

You said the costs involved in promoting individual local brands outweigh their potential profits, and most supermarket managers won't be bothered with brands they can't easily sell.

There's no question that getting shelf space for local ethnic packaged goods is a challenge. But until those goods get on the shelf, there's no way of knowing how profitable they can be to the merchant, the manufacturer and you, the distributor.

As a distributor, you know the cost-effectiveness in bundling like-kind product lines in shipping; why not use the same approach to in-store promotion and marketing?

As you can see from the enclosed material, I'm a specialist in selling ethnic goods to supermarket chains – from Chilean to Chinese. I've represented many local, regional and national brands, helping to turn unknown lines into household staples through cost-effective promotional programs.

Mr. Bigg, I have some ideas that may appeal to you and your manufacturers, and I'll call you next week to discuss them with you. Thank you for your time, and I'm looking forward to speaking with you.

Score: I's: 5 You's: 12

Comments: This letter makes it easy for Mr. Bigg to realize this applicant not only has a feel for his dilemma with his ethnic products, but is already formulating strategies to move his merchandise. Notice the structure of the letter:

Paragraphs One and Two: Although the applicant is simply repeating what Mr. Bigg said in the article, he comes across as an expert in selling small ethnic brands to supermarkets – without having to say that he was one.

Paragraph Three: By briefly discussing the problem and/or opportunity Mr. Bigg faces with small ethnic brands, the applicant implies he already has an understanding of Mr. Bigg's concerns.

Paragraph Four: By suggesting a way to help Mr. Bigg address this issue, the applicant acts as if he is already working for Mr. Bigg. Notice that no specific ideas are given; only a vague reference to "bundling" and "in-store promotion and marketing."

Paragraphs Five: By now, Mr. Bigg is thinking, "Who are you?" The applicant intentionally downplays his track record to get Mr. Bigg to read his resume, which he does to learn more about the ethnic-brands expert he's going to meet.

Paragraph Six: The applicant makes it very clear he:

◆ Expects to meet with Mr. Bigg soon; by assuming responsibility for follow-up, he proves he is responsible, thorough, detail-oriented and capable, which Mr. Bigg would expect of anyone he hires, and

◆ Is already mapping out a game plan for Mr. Bigg's ethnic lines so he can hit the ground selling.

This applicant will have no problem getting hired by Mr. Bigg or a comparable company; good talent like this is hard to find.

Letter #2: Could You Be a Little More Vague?
I would like to be considered as a case manager with United Cerebral Palsy of Tarrant County. I have been a licensed social worker for 12 years, and my experience has been assisting a diverse population with a variety of issues.

My job responsibilities required me to work with multiple agencies and in a team setting so that organizational skills were a must. In each position, I have had to display independent think-ing and initiative, taking on greater and greater responsibilities.

Generally, I am an intelligent, dependable, conscientious, hard-working individual who possesses a great desire to learn new things and acquire new skills. I think I would add greatly to your organization in this position. I look forward to hearing from you.

Score: I's: 10 You's: 3

Comments: Case managers are social workers or registered nurses who help patients and their families find community resources to meet their specific needs. At a large nonprofit agency like UCP, this position is critical to serving its special-needs clientele, yet you wouldn't know it from this letter.

The applicant never mentions what services UCP provides to its special-needs clientele. All she can think about is getting what she wants, not what UCP or its clients want.

Letter #2 Rewrite: What Can I Do to Help?

I understand United Cerebral Palsy of Tarrant County is expand-ing its outreach in the community, which is welcome news to your clients and their families who depend on the wide variety of services you provide.

What most people don't realize is that UCP serves many people with disabilities unrelated to Cerebral Palsy, including autism, post polio and Alzheimer's.

And they may not know about your Client Intervention Program, which provides access to a wide variety of community resources to improve individual and family functioning and to encourage personal independence.

As a social worker for the past 12 years, I find that working with special-needs clients and their families is one of the most rewarding things a clinician can do. If I can help make it easier for a family to care for their loved ones or for clients to care for themselves, that's all that matters.

Mr. Bigg, please take a few minutes to look at my information, and I'll give you a call next week to discuss how we might work together to increase UCP's presence in the community. Thank you for your time, and I'm looking forward to speaking with you.

Score I's: 6 You's: 11

Comments: This social worker's heartfelt compassion for her clients comes across clearly, as does her knowledge about the work of the agency, which she got simply by reading its website.

Mr. Bigg will want to meet or at least get to know this sincere and experienced clinician. If he can't hire her at UCP, he knows many agencies and hospitals that can.

Letter #3: Waiting For My One Big Chance
(Written as a template)

I am interested in applying for the junior broker position mentioned on your website. After viewing your website and reading your firm's goals and ideals, I felt as though I was tailor-made for this position.

I believe my leadership qualities and interpersonal skills would be of great use to [Some Company]. I have had extensive course studies in finance and business as referenced in my resume, and am goal-oriented, as well as having a strong background of working in teams.

I believe both these qualities could have a great positive effect on your day-to-day operations. [Some Company] is a top-notch financial company, known for its professionalism, in addition to its success.

I would like a chance to use my traits of diligence and dedication to work at [Some Company]. I have a strong history of leadership and goals met and exceeded.

While studying business at college, I served as president, as well as treasurer, of Greek Girls Sorority. During this time, I initiated a scholarship fund with funding in excess of $250,000.

I also spearheaded the largest philanthropy on campus during my senior year, raising over $25,000 for the local Food

Finders food bank.

I believe my fundraising and creative marketing approaches would be a great benefit to [Some Company]. I am anxious to talk with you and discuss my potential to contribute to your organization.

I plan to call you in three days to schedule a meeting. You can reach me at (444) 123-5555 or by email at iwannajob@collegiatecollege.com.

Score: I's: 21 You's: 12

Comments: This new graduate is very eager to impress, but doesn't understand that while her undergraduate charity and scholarship fundraising efforts were wonderful for the good they did, they have no relevance to working as a junior broker at a financial services firm.

Her "extensive course studies" didn't teach her that the business of a nonprofit is serving people, while the business of a financial brokerage concern is making money from investing other people's money.

However, if she had wanted to do fundraising, membership enrollment or marketing for a foundation or nonprofit agency, then those collegiate experiences would definitely count.

So, what do you do when you don't have much or any real-world training and/or experience, and believe you have to prove yourself just to get started? You get creative.

Letter #3 Rewrite: I'm Not Much, But I'm All I've Got
(Written to Mr. Bigg)

In your position as Manager of Broker Development for Imperial Financial Services, you know how important it is to make sure your customers are not only pleased with your company's services, but will be happy enough to refer their friends to you.

I understand Imperial Financial has a new program designed to help small business owners leverage their capital through a review of their tangible assets.

Although this program is modeled on your highly successful corporate asset review program, it is tailored to the unique needs of small business owners and is bound to be a huge success.

My father has been an entrepreneur for 20 years, and I know he and other members of the local Chambers of Commerce and other business groups in this area would be very interested to learn about your new program.

Perhaps I can help you market this program to the small business owners you want to reach. As you can see from the attached material, I've just graduated with a degree in finance and marketing, and have worked with groups of people in various financial marketing positions.

Mr. Bigg, I have some ideas how to promote your small business program at the grass roots level, and I'll call you next week to discuss a few of them with you. Thank you for your time, and I'm looking forward to speaking with you.

Score: I's: 8 You's: 19

Comments: This new college graduate knows there's no way she can compete with older, more experienced MBA's for a junior broker position, so she doesn't try. Instead, she creates a niche within Mr. Bigg's company that only she can fill.

By offering herself as a "feet on the street" presenter of this new program to small, local business owners who are under the radar of Mr. Bigg's current marketing efforts, she supplements and complements his existing program for larger clients.

Is Mr. Bigg favorably impressed? You bet: here is someone who is obviously smart, can get things done on her own initiative and is ready to start making him money. How lucky can he get?

Tell You What I'm Gonna Do...

One of the biggest pitfalls of the Traditional System is the belief that you can lure Mr. Bigg into wanting to see you by telling him what you can do for him. One website suggests:

"Say something like, 'Here's what I will bring to/can offer [company] as a [position],' and start describing the benefits they'd receive in hiring you. It tells them right away why you're writing and brings you immediately to communicating the value you offer."

The Traditional System says you should position yourself as the answer to Mr. Bigg's prayers just like these applicants do:

"I offer outstanding organizational skills, which are critical in developing, testing and maintaining mission-critical systems. These assets, combined with my ability to deliver a quality product under time constraints, enable me to make a positive impact on your company."

"My strong initiative and exceptional organizational skills, combined with my ability to work well under pressure, will enable me to make a substantial contribution to your company."

"I offer a comprehensive knowledge of numerous investment tools and the ability to deliver products and services seamlessly to customers. My experience, combined with my dedication and enthusiasm, should enable me to make an immediate and valuable impact on your company."

"I can contribute quickly to your success. My experience is technical, non-technical, hands-on and strategic. I have thrived in fast-paced environments and know the value of good planning, flexibility and understandable priorities. My enthusiastic approach and hands-on style will benefit you in ways you can't even predict."

For the sake of your career, it is essential you realize that when you tell Mr. Bigg what you will do for him, you are actually:

◆ Making a promise you will be required to fulfill,
◆ Setting a standard that you will be expected to meet, and worst of all, and
◆ Insulting him by implying:
  "Despite your many years of experience in this industry, in-depth expertise in this matter, long tenure with this company and first-

hand knowledge of this situation, you are inept, incompetent and incapable of coming up with a solution to your problem. Fortunately for you, *I* am finally here."

Reality Check

It is the height of arrogance to assume you – a total stranger – have insight into Mr. Bigg's problem he doesn't, and that you know how to fix it. The only time you should give Mr. Bigg your opinion about his situation is when he asks you for it and/or you are being paid to give it to him.

CHAPTER TEN

Keeping the Ball in Play

*"God gives every bird its food,
but He does not throw it into the nest."*

– Josiah Gilbert Holland, Poet

THE BLACK HOLE

*"If email had been around before the telephone,
people would have said, 'Hey, forget email; with this
new telephone thing, I can actually talk to people.'"*

– Anonymous

So now you've mailed off your letter and resume; what happens next? Usually nothing, and this is the most frustrating part of the Traditional System because you've done everything you're supposed to do, and now all you can do is wait.

You can handle rejection; it's the feeling that you don't even rate a response that irks you. Of course you're upset; you've bought into the Traditional System belief that simply as a matter of courtesy, Mr. Bigg should acknowledge receipt of your resume and let you know if he's interested in you or not.

Because Mr. Bigg doesn't contact you, you probably assume he's not interested in you. Nothing could be further from the truth; in fact, he's probably wondering why you haven't called!

Reality Check

It is your responsibility to follow up with Mr. Bigg after you've sent him your resume; it is not his responsibility to follow up with you.

One Ringy Dingy

You may be leery about calling because you're afraid Mr. Bigg will say "no" and you'll be embarrassed, or the ad you saw said "No calls," but most of all, you don't call because you probably don't know what to say.

No wonder. The Traditional System has scant advice on how to do follow up, and what little there is falls into four categories:

The Pitch: This is where you "sell yourself" using an elevator speech or 30-second commercial.

The Prod: Getting past the gatekeeper is considered a major challenge. How can you sell yourself to the boss if his secretary won't put you through or you keep getting voice mail?

The Push: Once you're on the phone with Mr. Bigg, you're determined to get that meeting, no matter how much he resists.

The Pinch: In this pre-interview screening phone call, you will either be winnowed out of the running or be invited to a face-to-face meeting. Since no Contrarian System job seeker will ever encounter The Pinch, it will not be discussed.

The Pitch

According to the Traditional System, your elevator speech or 30-second commercial is a concise statement of who you are, what you want and what you offer. You're supposed to whip this out when you meet someone so they know who you are and why they should want to know you better:

> "My name is Chris Stanley and I generated a 30% increase in territory sales over the past six months. Additionally, I developed a product projection matrix that has increased product diversification among our client physicians by 15% over a two-month time period. My ultimate goal is to use my industry knowledge to increase the profitability of a cutting-edge company."

"Hi, I'm Joe Smith. I'm an award-winning, $1.3 million-a-year sales executive with 15 years of telecommunications industry experience. Are you in need of a top-producing professional with extensive industry connections and vendor contacts plus impeccable negotiation and sales-closing skills?"

"I'm Tim Brody. I'm a creative business person with expertise in human resource management in organizations undergoing significant change. I have helped several high-tech companies achieve their business goals by developing effective human capital practices.

"I also built an HR consulting business that helps small organizations attain their strategic goals. I like helping people create successful, effective organizations. I am seeking an executive position where I can use my expertise and business acumen to improve long-term business success."

"I'm Jack Ross, a senior in finance at UB. Last summer, I interned with Smith Financial, and because of my strong analytical skills and ability to communicate with clients, they asked me to continue with them this fall, redesigning their service demonstrations for the entire Northeast.

"This was valuable training because it gave me greater insight into the finance industry, allowed me to show my ability as a team player and confirmed my desire to become an analyst for a top-ten firm such as yours. Could you tell me how my experience and education may be useful to you?"

Reality Check

When you give an elevator speech, you are pitching yourself *at* Mr. Bigg, not talking *to* him, and certainly not having a conversation *with* him. Elevator speeches are like summaries of qualifications because they're all about how wonderful you think you are, and instead of attracting people, you're actually alienating them.

So can the canned speech. When you meet someone and want them to like you, say as little about yourself as possible. Just state your name, briefly mention what you do, and then shift the conversation back to them and keep it focused on them. This is called reverse psychology, and it works like a charm:

"I'm Janet White and I sell patient-care equipment for the obese to hospitals. What do you do?"

"I'm Ray Rogers and I'm an industrial real estate broker. And what do you do?"

"Great to meet you, John. I'm Leo Mini and I help people find their dream homes without making the process a nightmare. What do you do?"

"I'm glad to know you, Peter. I'm with a start-up design company and we're doing a new project you might be interested in. Do you have a few minutes?"

The Prod

This is it. You've sent off your resume and letter, and now you've braced yourself for what could be the most important phone call of your life. You gather up all of your courage, take a deep breath and punch the number, determined to speak to Mr. Bigg.

Susan: "John Bigg's office, this is Susan."

Uh, oh, it's the secretary. You've got to get past her to get a shot at Mr. Bigg.

You: "Is Mr. Bigg in?"

Susan: "He's in a meeting. Who's calling?"

You: "I'm Steve Thomas, and I want to talk to Mr. Bigg about the position you advertised for an analyst." (You launch into your 30-second commercial.)

Susan (interrupting): "If this is about a job, you'll have to speak to Human Resources. I'll transfer you."

If your follow-up calls go something like this, then you've bought into the Traditional System myth that a secretary's job is act as a buffer between her boss and the rest of the world. Take it from someone who spent five years as a secretary – rather than being an obstacle, the secretary can be your biggest ally, if you treat her right.

The Truth About Secretaries

If you've ever been a secretary or clerical worker, you know what the job is like. If you haven't, you should appreciate that for the most part, it stinks. Essentially, you are invisible unless someone wants something, and you are thought of as nothing more than a pair of hands with a brain attached, one that you are not expected to use much.

Your opinion is not sought and does not count. People who are right in front of you talk around you as if you do not exist, and your only authority is to order lunch or office supplies. You are not expected to read or care about what you're typing or filing, you are easily replaced by a temp, and people are shocked if you express any kind of ambition.

That being said, for many professional secretaries and administrative assistants, their work is a source of pride, especially if they work with senior corporate executives at large companies.

But for the vast majority of clerical workers, especially those who yearn not to be one, it can be a secure but degrading job. If you can type fast and accurately enough, you can always get work to pay your bills and get your ego soothed elsewhere.

Knowing this, your best tactic is to treat the secretary as an intelligent resource, rather than as an obstacle to circumvent. You want her on your side because she can be your biggest help or worst hindrance.

Reality Check

There is one sure-fire way to make the secretary your ally from your very first call: just use her name and then ask her a favor.

Susan: "John Bigg's office, this is Susan."

You: "Susan, I wonder if you can help me. My name is Steve Thomas, and I sent John some information last week. Do you know if he got it?"

When you treat the secretary with respect and dignity, she will give you all kinds of useful information:

◆ Susan is a temp or is filling in for John's secretary, so she doesn't see his mail.

◆ Susan is John's secretary, but she doesn't screen his mail.

◆ Susan does or does not screen his mail but says John's been on vacation, out sick, out of town, preparing for a big meeting, etc. Your material is still on his desk, unopened.

◆ Susan does or does not screen John's mail but says John said you should talk to Mary Small, the Vice President of Data Analysis, and she'll transfer you.

◆ Susan does or does not screen John's mail but says John wants to see you. Can you come in next week?

If Susan says, "What was the material about?" tell her exactly what you would tell Mr. Bigg, should he ask you that same question (see "I Didn't Get It" below.)

Since Susan won't be able to respond to what you ask her, she'll either put you through to Mr. Bigg or someone else who can. Remember, if Mr. Bigg is going to be your boss, you're going to be working with Susan, so having a good relationship with her from the outset is essential.

The Game
When I was a secretary, I had a game I played with callers: anyone who took the time and trouble to learn my name and use it got right

through to my boss, and anyone who didn't . . . didn't.

When callers used my name, they saw me as a fellow human being, and treated me as a colleague and peer, and so I went out of my way to help them. Here's a typical conversation with someone who knows how to treat the secretary right:

Janet: "John Bigg's office; this is Janet."

Lee: "Hi Janet, this is Lee Brown from Leasing International. You must be John's new assistant; it's nice to meet you. I'll stop by to see you the next time I visit."

Janet: "I'd like that, Lee. Oh, hold on. John just got back into his office. Here he is."

The next time Lee calls, the conversation goes like this:

Janet: "John Bigg's office; this is Janet."

Lee: "Hi, Janet, it's Lee Brown from Leasing International. How are you doing?"

Janet: "Hi, Lee. I'm good. How are you?"

Lee: "I'm great but I have something important to discuss with John. Is he free?"

Janet: "I'd put you through, but he's with a client right now."

Lee: "Could you do me a big favor and ask him to call me when he gets a chance?"

Janet: "You bet, Lee. I'll slip him a note that it's urgent."

Lee: "Thanks, Janet. Have a good day."

Janet: "Any time, Lee. Goodbye."

By using my name and treating me like a human being, Lee has gained my trust. Notice that Lee never told me what he wanted to talk to my boss about, and I didn't ask. But any time Lee calls, he will use my name, and I will do my best to help him.

The Push

According to Monster.com: The goal of a phone contact is to get an interview. To succeed, you must be ready to get past the first and even the second rejection:

You: "When may I come in for an interview?"

Employer: "I don't have any positions open now . . ."

You: "That's okay. I'd still like to come in to talk to you about the possibility of future openings."

Employer: "I don't plan on hiring for six months or so."

You: "Then I'd like to come in and learn more about what you do. You know a lot about the industry, and I'm looking for ideas on getting into it and moving up."

Monster.com says that although this approach does not always work, asking the third time works more often than most people would believe! It is important to learn to do this, since overcoming initial rejections is a very important part of getting to 'yes'.

If by some remote chance you do get a meeting using this approach, it will be simply because you wore down Mr. Bigg's resistance by sheer force, and he only agreed to see you to get rid of you.

You completely ignored the fact that another person with his own priorities was involved in this conversation, and Mr. Bigg's first and most important impression of you is that you are selfish, pushy and arrogant.

Thanks to the aggressive tactics of the Traditional System, Mr. Bigg now considers you a world-class pest, will most likely have his assistant cancel the meeting, and your chances of working for Mr. Bigg at any time are just about zero.

Voice Mail

"This is John Bigg. I'm not in, so leave a message and I'll call you back."

So you leave a message:

"Mr. Bigg, this is Robin Sloan. I sent you my resume last week about the analyst position posted on your website. I believe I have the exact qualifications you are looking for. Please call me at 222-555-1212."

A week goes by and he doesn't call, so you try it again:

"Mr. Bigg, this is Robin Sloan again. I left you a message last week to follow up about my resume for the analyst position. Could you let me know if you've had a chance to review my qualifications? I have re-emailed you my resume in case you didn't get the first one. You can call me at 222-555-1212. Thank you."

You let another week go by, and with gritted teeth and a sinking feeling, you try it one last time:

"Mr. Bigg, this is Robin Sloan again. I know you must be very busy not to return phone calls, and I'm hoping the analyst position is still open. I just want five minutes of your time to discuss my qualifications and to show you how suitable I am for the position.

"I know I can do a superior job for you. Please let me know when I can come in and see you. My number is 222-555-1212. Thank you."

You never hear from Mr. Bigg or anyone at that company, and with a sigh, you toss the ad in the trash. Why didn't Mr. Bigg call you back? It could be any number of reasons:

- He's on vacation or a business trip, is out sick, is getting ready to go on vacation or a business trip, or has left the company and forgot to change his voice mail.

- He's working on a major project or is putting out fires, and everything else is lost in the shuffle.

- He's not the most organized person; his desk is a giant mess and your messages are probably in there somewhere.

- He is head of the department, but analysts have their own supervisor. He can't be bothered talking to people who don't do their homework.

- The position's been filled internally and he hopes that if he ignores you, you'll get the message intuitively and stop bothering him, which you eventually do.

✓ Reality Check

Leave one follow-up voice mail with Mr. Bigg, and call back one week later. If you're still getting voice mail, don't leave another message and don't assume this means anything.

Instead, hit "0" – chances are you will get a live person. If the phone system is so convoluted you can't get a live person, hit an extension for a department that will answer, like sales or accounting, and ask whoever answers how to reach Mr. Bigg.

Once in a while, there is no live operator and no one answers the phone at all. If this happens, ask yourself if you want to work for a company that makes it so difficult to contact them. After all, if you can't get through, neither can their customers – that is, if they have any left.

Conversely, voice mail may be the only way to reach someone who travels a lot, and most people on the road check their voice mail daily. Because of their schedules, even though they are getting your messages, they may not be able to call you back any time soon, so don't take delays personally. Also remember that you are not a priority to them.

Many job applicants fail to realize there is a very fine line between staying in touch and being a pest. Leave a maximum of two voice mails over three weeks, and if you're still not getting a response, let this one go. There are plenty of other companies who will want you, so don't waste your time chasing after one that doesn't.

But if you've reached Mr. Bigg or his secretary and been told to call back, when should you call again? Don't guess; just ask: "When would you suggest I get back in touch with you?" and they will tell you. Then it will be up to you to make that call because they'll be expecting your call.

OMG! It's Him!

Good secretaries are so scarce these days that most people in authority answer their own phones, and besides, many executives don't want anyone screening their calls for them. So be prepared to hear, "John Bigg" when you dial his number.

The Traditional System says that when you get Mr. Bigg on the phone, you're supposed to tell him you're applying for a job and then launch into your elevator speech. Let's say you're a special education teacher with a long, successful track record in working with autistic children.

You're now burned out on teaching, and figure you'd be great selling for a manufacturer or distributor of special educational toys, books and teaching materials. You have no sales experience or training, but you know you'd be perfect for this job; you just have to convince the company's sales manager of that.

John (answering his phone): "John Bigg."

You: "Mr. Bigg, my name is Stephanie Murphy, and I am a former special education teacher who specializes in working with autistic children. I'm looking for a job selling special education toys and education materials to school districts.

"With 20 years experience and a master's degree in special

education, I have an unparalleled insight into the unique needs of these children. I believe I would make an ideal addition to your sales force."

According to the Traditional System, your elevator speech, combined with a strong pitch for a job, is supposed to wow Mr. Bigg into wanting to see you. Unfortunately, this approach almost always backfires:

John: "That may be true, but right now we're full up with salespeople. Why don't you send me your resume and keep in touch. Thanks for calling."

Reality Check

If you pitch yourself at Mr. Bigg by using an elevator speech, you can expect to be off the phone within a few minutes and never know why.

I Didn't Get It

Should you be at all concerned about talking to Mr. Bigg on the phone, write out your greeting so when he answers, you can respond without pitching, hustling or panicking, like this:

"Mr. Bigg, this is Stephanie Murphy, and I'm calling to follow up on some material I sent you last week. Did you have a chance to look it over?"

The chances are good that even if he got your material, he probably didn't read it and it's on the Someday-I'll-Get-To-It pile.

Reality Check

If Mr. Bigg didn't get your material, or didn't read it, or wants to know what it was about or you have to leave a voice mail, what do you talk about if not yourself? Remember his problem or opportunity you discussed in your cover letter? *That's* what you talk about!

Here's how your Contrarian phone call goes:

John: "John Bigg."

You: "Mr. Bigg, this is Stephanie Murphy, and I'm calling to follow up on some material I sent you last week. Did you have a chance to look it over?"

John: "I don't recall getting anything from you. What was it about?"

You: "I understand your firm is launching a new line of therapeutic toys for autistic children, and I was wondering if you had considered marketing these toys to pediatric therapists and special education teachers as well as to parents. Are you familiar with play therapy?"

John: "Yes, of course."

You: "Then you know the key to a successful program is matching the right toys with the child's needs. Much of the time, a therapist can readily design an effective program with out-of-the-box toys.

"But autistic children are often noncommunicative, may have difficulty socializing with others and are extremely sensitive to light, sound and touch. Regular toys just won't suffice for these children.

"That's why I wanted to talk with you about your new therapeutic toys. They are desperately needed, and perhaps I can help you get them to the teachers and therapists you want to reach.

"I spent many years teaching autistic children, and I know a lot of specialists who would want to evaluate the effectiveness of your products with these children."

John: "Perhaps you can help us. We've been in the toy business a long time, but we've never done anything like this before. We sure could use someone with your insight. Can you come in next week to talk to us?"

JACKPOT! Mr. Bigg has convinced himself you can help him and is eager to see you. And you did all this without him reading your resume, selling yourself, allowing yourself to be interrogated or being the least bit nervous.

Reality Check

The key to a successful follow-up call is to never forget this call is not about you; it's about Mr. Bigg. The instant it becomes about you, Mr. Bigg will know he's being hustled, cut the phone call short and cut you out of his life.

Let's Keep Talking

It may happen you will talk with Mr. Bigg before you send him anything, such as when you get a referral and been told to call right away, see something timely and want to take immediate action, or are very good on the phone.

Your follow-up email then is a variation of a cover letter, but it's easier to write because you already know Mr. Bigg's situation:

Subject Line: Seismic Mapping

Dear Alan,

It was a pleasure speaking with you today about your challenges in keeping up with the latest mapping technology, and for sharing that you want to immediately begin seismic mapping of your recently acquired properties.

As you mentioned, the faster you accelerate your exploration schedule, the faster you can write down your company's debt and can pour the profits back into your company.

That's why I thought you would be interested in knowing about some unique strategies I've developed that may increase your ability to find productive well sites. As you can see from the attached material, I've been doing just this for many years for other companies.

Alan, thank you for your time this morning, and I'll see you on August 17th at 2 p.m. Have a great day.

Score: I's: 4 You's: 16

Comments: It was a great phone call and this letter confirms it will be a great meeting for both of them.

CHAPTER ELEVEN

The Blind Date

"The road to success is always under construction."

– Lily Tomlin, Comedienne

WHAT! ME WORRY?

"I am always doing things I can't do.
That's how I get to do them."

– Pablo Picasso

I t's the cumulation of weeks or months of sending resumes, making phone calls and talking to everyone you know. This is your one big chance to get this job, and everything rides on this meeting.

Congrats! Somehow you've landed an interview with a person in Human Resources whom you have never met before and will probably never meet again, but who is the linchpin to your getting hired at this company.

To prepare for this meeting, you've studied dozens of websites and books on how to interview, and even though they contain conflicting and often confusing advice, you're ready to knock 'em dead no matter what the HR person throws at you.

And that's the problem: it's like you've been cramming for an important exam, but you don't know what to study, so you have to be ready for anything and everything, including one or more of these kinds of Traditional System interviews:

The Sieve: You're a bit worried about that gap on your resume you have to explain away and you really don't really fit their requirements, but you can make a good case that your skills and experience are transferable . . . you hope. If the meeting goes well and you have a bit of luck, you might even make it to the next round.

The Audition: Since you're going for a sales job, you expect to be told something like, "Sell me this pen" and you have your pitch all ready, especially the one about yourself.

The Behavioral Interview: They'll want to know how you handled difficult situations in other jobs by asking you such sticky questions as:

◆ Describe a situation in which you forced yourself to finish an assignment or task that you did not want to do.

◆ What was the worst decision you ever made, and what were the positive and negative consequences of that decision? What did you learn from it?

◆ Tell me about a time when you missed an obvious solution to a problem.

◆ Give a specific example of a policy you conformed to that you didn't agree with.

◆ By providing examples, convince me you can adapt to a wide variety of people, situations and environments.

◆ Describe an instance when you had to think on your feet to extricate yourself from a difficult situation.

The Panel Interview: You'll be grilled by different people at the same time, so you've practiced how to answer a question from one person while looking at another. You can handle the questions; it's the silent, stone-faced responses that throw you.

Multiple Interviews: You have to see several people at the company, so they've booked you back-to-back with meetings on the same day. Your big concern is if they ask you the same questions and then compare your answers. What if you say something different to different people?

You've also prepped yourself to be ready for one or more of the four identifiable kinds of Traditional System interviewers:

The Drill Sergeant: This no-nonsense person will adhere to a rigid agenda and fire a lot of questions at you. Although you'll probably feel steamrolled, you're ready for an overtly domineering questioner.

The Analyst: To get to know you really well, this interviewer will ask you deep, personal questions that probe you psychologically, like:

- What are your long- and short-range goals and objectives? When and why did you establish these goals and how are you preparing yourself to achieve them?
- What did you want to be when you were ten years old?
- What part of the newspaper do you turn to first?
- How will taking this job change your life?
- What would I find in your refrigerator?
- What does it take to get under your skin?

The Joker: This interviewer will ask you questions to determine how you reason, even though there is no reason to do so:

- What does all the ice in a hockey rink weigh?
- Why are manhole covers round?
- How would you design a spice rack for a blind person?
- What is the temperature when it's twice as cold as zero?
- How many quarters, placed one top of the other, would it take to reach the top of the Empire State Building?

The Cross Examiner: First, they intentionally make you wait for an hour just to get you anxious. Then they use intimidation to shake your confidence by staring at you silently, being sullen, challenging your beliefs, interrupting you, turning their backs on you, sighing at your answers, rolling their eyes and intentionally mishearing, misunderstanding or belittling you.

You know you're being tested to see how you react under stress and how well you can keep your emotions under control. You also know you're expected to respond calmly, coolly and rationally to such degrading comments as:

- What can compensate for your lack of experience and education in this field?
- You seem too timid to handle these responsibilities.
- That is the worst answer we've heard yet from any of the candidates.
- I don't see any evidence you have what it takes to succeed in this field.

You know it's nothing personal, but it will be all you can do to just sit there and take it. So, to prepare yourself for whatever happens, you memorize pat answers to the top 500 interview questions including:

- How do you make important decisions?
- Tell us about your morals and integrity.
- Why should we hire you?
- What have you been doing since you left your last job?
- What have your last three evaluations said about you?
- What can you tell me in five minutes that would persuade me to hire you?
- Why did you choose that major?
- If you had the last ten years of your life to live over again, what would you do differently?
- How would you describe the essence of success?

And the #1 worst Traditional System interview question of all time: TELL ME ABOUT YOURSELF.

Reality Check

You can never answer Traditional System interview questions correctly because there are no correct answers. The best you can hope for is what you said pleased the interviewer and was what they wanted to hear.

If you do get hired, you may never know if you said the right thing or just got lucky. If you don't get hired, you'll never know what it was you said or did or didn't say or do that made them take a pass on you.

Reality Check:

A Traditional System job interview is an intimidating, intrusive and irrelevant personal interrogation that should never be tolerated.

Your Meeting or Mine?

According to the Traditional System, this nerve-wracking, ulcer-causing, gut-wrenching event is supposed to be the highlight of your job search. The HR person who has been making you sweat allegedly has all the power, control and authority to:

♦ Determine whether your personality will fit in the company (even though you probably won't work with or for that individual and most likely will never see them again),
♦ Permit you to actually talk to Mr. Bigg, or
♦ Decide you don't have what it takes.

The Traditional System teaches that if you don't get past Human Resources, you'll never get on the company's payroll. Fortunately, what you've been taught is wrong.

Reality Check

Mr. Bigg is the only person who can hire you, so he is the only person you should talk to or meet with. To ace your interview with Mr. Bigg, you only have to remember one thing and remember it throughout your meeting: this meeting is *not* about you.

The meeting is really about Mr. Bigg, and he's trying to determine if you can help him solve his problem. He has a problem, and to a very large degree, he already believes you can help him solve it – if he didn't believe that, he wouldn't be wasting his time talking to you.

So relax. You're halfway home to getting hired just by getting the meeting!

How Does It Fit?

Once you realize the meeting is not about you and Mr. Bigg is on your side, there is no reason for you to be anxious. The worst that can happen is Mr. Bigg refers you to someone else to talk to either at his company or somewhere else, so whether or not he hires you, you win.

In fact, it is Mr. Bigg who is under the gun, not you. You have your pick of employers, but Mr. Bigg is in a bind and, contrary to what the Traditional System will tell you, he really doesn't have much of a choice who he can hire.

Unless you are going for a job that anyone with routine skills can do, there just aren't that many local, available, qualified people at any given time who:

- Can do what Mr. Bigg needs done,
- Who Mr. Bigg knows about that he can contact,
- Who are aware that Mr. Bigg has a need for their services even if he posts an ad, or
- Who have the wherewithal to contact Mr. Bigg on their own.

Reality Check

The Traditional System claims the purpose of the interview is to see if you "fit" the organization. This is not correct. The real purpose of the interview is to see if you and Mr. Bigg "fit" each other. Like any blind date, this first meeting will determine if you two can begin to have a relationship that will benefit both of you . . . or not.

Mr. Bigg needs someone who knows something about his problem, and he will hire the first person who he believes can solve it for him, which could easily be you. Since you both choose who you work with, why not choose to work with someone you like and who likes you?

An Interview Horror Story

In 1984, I was interviewed by the senior vice president of one of New York's leading public relations agencies, which had a very large and prestigious commercial real estate clientele.

By then, I had earned a master's degree in urban planning from New York University and had six years of experience in commercial real estate. I had been a journalist and publicist since high school, and was already writing about commercial real estate for a local trade group. If anyone was qualified to work as a commercial real estate writer and publicist, it was me.

As I waited for my meeting, one of the agency's account executives told me this was a terrible company and I should run before I agreed to work there. Hmmm.

"Peter" ran the agency's commercial real estate business, and I was there at his invitation. My resume was on his desk as I walked into his office, but it was full of large red marks – almost like a failing test being graded by a teacher.

Peter hadn't bothered with my portfolio of published articles, seemed annoyed I was there, and began firing questions at me the instant I sat down:

Peter: "Have you ever done a press conference?"
Janet: "No."
Peter: "Have you ever used a Blue Book?"
Janet: "No."
Peter: "Have you ever done crisis management?"
Janet: "No."

By this time, Peter was so angry that I was wasting his time that, without a word, he got up and walked out of his office. Obviously, the meeting was over, and I was never to darken his door again.

While Peter's unprofessional and boorish behavior guaranteed I would never work for him or that agency, I refused to tolerate his blatant attempt to intimidate and humiliate me.

So, since I had nothing better to do that afternoon, and Peter needed to be taught a lesson, I just sat there. After all, he had to come back to his office sometime.

Twenty minutes later, Peter came back whistling and was shocked to see me. Clearly, this was not the first time he had tried to crush someone's spirit to get rid of them, but it was the first time his cruel tactic didn't work, and this made him really mad.

What made him even madder was that I picked up the conversation exactly where he had dropped it, saying how I wanted to do public relations and writing only for commercial real estate, and not for the agency's other clients.

Infuriated, Peter stood up, clenched his fists on his desk and shouted at me, "YOU HAVE TO CHOOSE BETWEEN PR AND REAL ESTATE! YOU . . . CAN'T . . . HAVE . . . BOTH!"

So I stood up, clenched my fists on his desk and shouted at him, "WHY . . . NOT?"

And he shouted at me, "BECAUSE . . . YOU . . . CAN'T!"

With that, we sat down, and I calmly asked him, "Assuming I did go to work here, where do you see me? Churning out press releases with the new colleges graduates making $18,000 a year?"

Peter smirked, "Maybe making a little bit more than that."

I was 32, highly educated, had more direct experience in commercial real estate than most of his current staffers and was worth far more than chickenfeed, but not to him. With the meeting now officially over, I left, vowing I'd bake cookies for living before I ever worked for him or that agency.

Nobody tells me I can't do something when I know I can.

A few weeks later, I became Director of Public Relations for Landauer Associates, the most prestigious commercial real estate consulting and appraisal firm in the country, whose offices were several blocks from the public relations agency.

I was laid off from Landauer three years later, and immediately started my own commercial real estate public relations and writing business, eventually representing a wide variety of local, regional and national companies in New York and later Dallas.

I also became a very busy trade writer, doing feature articles under my own byline and ghost-writing articles for clients for many of the industry's top national magazines, including being New York editor for a Britsh-based international trade publication.

By the time I left real estate in 1996, I had been in the industry for eighteen years, had worked as a professional commercial real estate writer and publicist for twelve years, and had been in my own commercial real estate public relations and writing business nine years.

Peter was extremely wrong. I could indeed have both.

Turn Off the Heat

In a Traditional System interview, first you are interrogated, and then you get a chance to interrogate your interrogator. But while a lot of words are being spoken, there is no actual communication going on between the two of you, so you could have used email instead and saved yourself the trip.

Notice how these Traditional System interview questions you are supposed to ask employers are similar to the ones you are asked:

◆ What condition is morale in, and why?
◆ Does this company have a reactive or proactive approach to handling problems?
◆ What are the common satisfactions and frustrations of this job?
◆ Please describe your style of management.
◆ How does this position and department contribute to the company's overall mission and philosophy?
◆ How do you feel about creativity and individuality?
◆ How far into the future does the organization plan?
◆ What values are sacred to the company?

Reality Check

The Traditional System questions you are supposed to ask Mr. Bigg allegedly indicate your enthusiasm and interest in working for that company. In fact, they just make Mr. Bigg look foolish because, just like the questions he is supposed to ask you, there are no correct answers to your questions.

Of course you need certain kinds of information to decide if you want to work there, but it will only come from Mr. Bigg, and it won't come from interrogating him. It will come, however, from talking with him as if he were your peer and future colleague, because that's exactly what he is.

CHAPTER TWELVE

Meeting Mr. Bigg

"Eighty percent of success is showing up."

— *Woody Allen, Filmmaker*

IT'S NOT THE SAME OLD SONG

 "It's kind of fun to do the impossible."

– Walt Disney

Now you're finally going to meet Mr. Bigg. This may come as a shock to you, but you can totally control the meeting without him knowing it, starting when you walk in his office. There will be a greeting and a bit of small talk; if Mr. Bigg offers you a beverage, accept it even if you don't want it, don't like it and aren't thirsty.

> **Reality Check**
> When you accept a beverage, you instantly change the dynamics of the meeting: rather than being your hostile interrogator, Mr. Bigg is now a gracious host and you are his guest.

Take a sip of the beverage (or pretend to), and then get up and put it where you can't possibly spill it – like on his desk. That way, you can focus on Mr. Bigg, and not your drink.

Pull the Trigger
Now the pleasantries are over and you're both ready to get down to

business. But before Mr. Bigg can start to interrogate you, begin the conversation by asking him a "trigger question" or make a "trigger statement" that will get him talking about himself, his company and his situation.

Trigger questions should be based upon your research and knowledge about the company and industry, and sound something like:

- To a magazine editor: "That recent story you ran on high school entrepreneurs was terrific. Did you get a chance to try out some of their products?"

- To a commercial real estate developer (pointing to a rendering of a new project): "What a great looking building. How's the leasing going?"

- To an interior design firm: "It seems every time I open a paper, I read about hospitals expanding or new clinics being built. No wonder you've focused on this market."

- To a financial services director: "I read many new businesses are started by people in their 40's, 50's and even 70's. What a unique opportunity you have with them."

Reality Check

The more Mr. Bigg talks about whatever is important to him, the more likely it is he will talk himself right into hiring you.

Zip That Lip

Once you have asked your trigger question or made your trigger comment, don't say another word. Just sit there with a slight smile and wait for Mr. Bigg to respond, although he probably won't. Chances are he has never had an applicant talk so intelligently about his business before, and he will be shocked into silence.

This silence will probably last only a few minutes, but it may seem like hours. Regardless of how long it lasts or how strongly you feel the urge to say something – don't! Just sit there and wait for him to talk first; eventually, he will.

Reality Check

The instant Mr. Bigg breaks the silence and begins to talk, you have gained control of the meeting. You will stay in control as long as you keep Mr. Bigg talking, because whatever he talks about will be important to him and should immediately become important to you.

When Mr. Bigg starts to talk, he will launch into a monologue about himself and his company. You should then take out a small lined pad and start taking notes; these notes are very important and you will need them later.

Regardless of what Mr. Bigg is talking about, there will come a point when he will bring up whatever is most important to him. This is the real reason you are meeting with him, whether either of you knew it when you two arranged the meeting.

Reality Check

When you focus the meeting on Mr. Bigg, you will turn a tense interrogation between a supplicant job seeker and an omnipotent employer into a pleasant conversation between two peers.

When I was an independent publicist, my new client meetings went the same way as my job interviews: I would walk in, get Mr. Bigg to talk about himself and his company, and walk out with the business or the job. It was just that easy.

I'd ask a trigger question or make a trigger statement, and then shut up. Prompted by the silence, Mr. Bigg would start talking, continue to talk for 20 minutes (I have timed it), and finally say something like:

> "Now, Janet, when we have you working for us, the first thing we'll need you to do is _____" or "Our biggest problem with publicity is getting included in articles. Can you do that?"

This Stuff Works #1

When I was 25, I became Operations Assistant at WABC-AM in New York, fulfilling a lifelong dream. Since I was ten, I had longed to work at a radio station, and here I was, working at the flagship station of the American Broadcasting Company.

As I sat in my first music meeting, I thought, "I made it! I'm not just at any radio station; I'm at WABC – the number one radio station in America. How did I get here? *How* did I do this?"

How I did it was by using the Law of Attraction, even though back then I didn't know it existed. For years, I had seen myself working at a radio station, and one day, I was just in the right place at the right time.

Before joining WABC, I had been a secretary for a company in midtown Manhattan that sold commercial air time for independent radio stations. This was the closest I had come to actually being at a radio station, and I was chomping at the bit.

After five months at the sales agency, I felt inclined to tell Rob, one of the account executives, that I really wanted to work at a radio station, and I asked him if he knew anybody.

Rob said his best buddy was the program director of WABC, which was just a few blocks away. Rob then picked up the phone and called "Glenn" at WABC:

Rob: "Glenn, this is Rob. Listen, I got this great girl here and she really wants to work for a radio station. You got anything?"

Glenn: "Yes, and she'd better get down here right away because we're about to hire."

I met Glenn at the studio the next morning. He was three years older than I was but had been with WABC for six years. It turned out that Glenn was a local radio station junkie like me, so we spent our meeting talking about – what else? – local radio!

Although I had never worked at a radio station before, had no formal training in broadcasting, didn't even have a basic engineer's license, had no experience in radio production other than college radio which didn't count, and they had another candidate who knew what she was doing – I got the job.

Go figure.

This Stuff Works #2

As I wound down my public relations business in 1996, I went looking for clients. I was used to dealing with sophisticated companies at the upper edge of the industry, so my new clients had to have a corporate structure, deep financial pockets, a large, national, commercial real estate portfolio and be based in Dallas, where I now lived.

There were only a few companies that met my criteria, and the number two man at one of them agreed to see me. "Fred" headed the company's multi-family division, which was one of the largest apartment portfolios in the country at the time.

I had previously worked with one of Fred's biggest competitors, which had been sold to another company and merged into oblivion, so I was familiar with the kinds of issues Fred's company was most likely facing. Working for him seemed a natural fit.

Getting the meeting took some doing because Fred was traveling extensively inspecting some of their properties. After weeks of stalls and rescheduling through his secretary, I finally got my meeting.

But I didn't know why Fred had agreed to see me, since he and I had never spoken. In my letter to Fred, I explained that as a publicist, I had noticed his company was conspicuously absent in trade articles, industry reviews and opinion roundtables.

If his firm was anything like the other company I worked for, I guesstimated that Fred was going after large apartment management portfolio assignments from financial institutions like banks, insurance companies and pension funds.

Working under this assumption, I suggested to Fred that perhaps a bit of visibility in the trade press might help land some of these large accounts. Since I got the meeting, clearly, I had touched a nerve, but I didn't know if my guesstimate was true, or whether there was something else he needed help with.

After we shook hands, Fred apologized for the scheduling delays, saying he didn't get a chance to read my brochure because he just got back from a three-week trip.

We sat down with me on the sofa and him in a large, plush, executive chair, and there on his desk was his open briefcase with my brochure sticking up out of it. He hadn't read my brochure, but

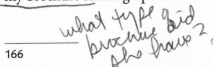

it was important enough for him to carry around for three weeks. Hmmm.

As we settled in, Fred leaned back in his chair, crossed his arms and legs, smiled and said, "I suppose you're here to tell me what you can do for me." Clearly, this was "Tell me about yourself," but I knew that would be a mistake for two reasons:

◆ Fred's body language was speaking volumes: he was leaning away from me and had crossed his arms and legs, mentally and physically raising a wall of resistance.

◆ I didn't know what he needed, so doing a "Here's What I Do and Why You Should Hire Me" sales pitch would be like throwing spaghetti against the wall and hoping some of it sticks.

Besides, in the nine years I was in business for myself, I had never done a sales pitch for anyone, and I wasn't about to do one for him. I would just go in, ask questions, actively listen, encourage Mr. Bigg to do all of the talking, and wait for the inevitable "yes."

This approach had always worked; Fred would be no different. But the first thing that had to happen was that Fred's wall of resistance had to come down. I decided to shatter it instead.

So, rather than allowing this meeting to be about me, I turned it around and made it about him by saying, "Actually, I'm here to listen. I want you to tell me how you think I can help you achieve your goals."

Fred's reaction was dramatic and instantaneous: his arms and legs flew apart, and he sat on the edge of his seat leaning forward with his eyes popping and his mouth hanging open. He had never gotten such a response from a vendor before, and his wall of resistance had simply vaporized; Fred was open, receptive and intrigued. *Now* we could have our meeting.

We sat in total silence for about three minutes when the pressure of the silence got to Fred, and he began to talk. He described at length how the company grew from a small, local property partnership to a national, mega-conglomerate with interests in every facet of commercial real estate.

Fred was right in the middle of discussing their industrial portfolio when he hit that magic 20-minute mark and right on cue, it happened. Completely out of the blue, totally off topic and from nowhere, Fred said, "One of the things I'm most proud of is our work in technology."

He then got up, walked over to his computer, and showed me Version 1.0 of a proprietary software program the company had built for its own portfolio. As I looked at it, I realized I was probably the first person outside the company to see this thing.

Being a non-techie, I couldn't care less about software, but since this was obviously very important to Fred, it became very important to me. Fred's excitement made it clear that this software program was more than a company project; it was his own personal baby, so I started treating him like the proud papa of a newborn, oooing and ahhing over his pride and joy:

"Would you look at that? Isn't that incredible! What else does it do? Have you made this available to your third-party owners? What do your managers think?"

The more I raved about his wonderful new software program, the more he beamed, so I poured it on. He then turned to me and said, "You know, we really need to tell people in the industry about this. You could do that for us, couldn't you?"

"Oh, yes," I said.

Fred got up, and smiling as he walked to his desk, he said, "I suppose when you walked in here, you didn't know you were walking out with two jobs, did you?"

Realizing he was teasing me because he was feeling good about hiring me, I went along with the joke, looked around and said, "Did I miss something?" Fred then handed me a piece of paper saying, "I was going to do this, but I think I'll let you handle it."

I walked out of that office with two assignments after spending an hour and a half with a man known to be impossible just to get in front of. And I never said one word about me.

And Over On Your Left . . .

In the Traditional System, your interview occurs in isolation behind a closed door, and you are shut off from everything and everyone else in the company. But if you want to show Mr. Bigg you really are interested in working for him, ask him to take you on a tour of the office, facility or plant.

Mr. Bigg should be flattered you asked and be glad to show you around, either right then or on your next visit. If he declines for no legitimate reason, this is a clear sign he's not convinced you're the right person for him or he's not the right person for you.

Should this happen, graciously end the meeting and be grateful you found out now that the vibes simply weren't right.

Reality Check

Mr. Bigg should be doing nearly all of the talking on your tour, especially about the company, its projects and its plans. Encourage him to keep talking about whatever is important to him, and be an interested, engaged listener, even if you have to fake it.

There is a very good chance that during your tour you will meet "Charlie," one of Mr. Bigg's employees; you are "Diane." Out of sheer politeness, Mr. Bigg will be inclined to introduce you:

Mr. Bigg: "Charlie, I want you to meet Diane. Diane's going to be helping us with our new program."

You: "Nice to meet you, Charlie."

Congratulations, you have just been hired. Wasn't that easy?

By greeting Charlie, you have accepted the job, and Mr. Bigg, who is congratulating himself on his ability to hire great people, proceeds to introduce you to more of your new co-workers.

Reality Check

Going on a tour gives Mr. Bigg an opportunity to introduce you to other people in the company, and he will most likely introduce you as a new employee.

If Mr. Bigg takes you around and does not introduce you, this is a very good indication he's not that serious about you. Chances are, you were probably not serious about him either, so it's no loss. But the odds are in your favor if you go on a tour and keep Mr. Bigg talking about himself and his company, you'll go home with a job.

If this scenario has never happened to you, it may be hard for you to imagine that getting hired could be so easy and effortless. Remember the Law of Attraction: whatever you believe to be true will manifest in your life to reflect your belief.

So, if you want to have an "impossible" hiring scenario like this, you first have to release your doubts, fears, and assumptions about what is supposed to happen. But if you can't let them go and are convinced this situation is not realistic and could never happen to you, you're right; it won't.

The Firing Squad

The Traditional System has specific advice about how to handle the dreaded panel interview in which you are grilled by two or more interrogators:

> "Get a feel for the group's dynamics and keep communication lines open by periodically making eye contact with all panel members as you respond to questions. Deliver honest and thoughtful answers, maintaining a certain level of energy and enthusiasm.

> "Speak clearly and loudly enough for all the panel members to hear what you say. Direct an answer primarily to the person who asked the question, but look at the others from time to time and be alert to any reactions from them (nods of approval, etc.)."

This "advice" is simply common sense. Of course you would make eye contact as you clearly and enthusiastically deliver honest and thoughtful answers with a lot of energy loudly enough so they all can hear you while focusing on the person who asked the question. Why wouldn't you?

Reality Check

Treat each panel member like an individual Mr. Bigg, because that's exactly what they are.

Everything you've learned about dealing with Mr. Bigg one-on-one applies to a panel interview, because each panel member has their own individual agendas, issues and concerns.

This Stuff Works #3

When I was an independent publicist, a national commercial real estate company was interested in having me work for them. I was to be interviewed by the heads of the company's four divisions and two other senior-level field people in a single meeting. The CEO was not there, but would agree to whatever the panel recommended.

The executives were in Dallas for a corporate meeting, and I was to meet them for dinner after their business day was over. Two of the executives were local, so they asked me to meet all of them at a family pizza restaurant close to where one of them lived (no joke).

I sat at the corner of the table facing the heads of the office, apartment, industrial and retail divisions – four different kinds of income-producing, investment-grade properties, none of which had anything in common with each other.

As we were being served our food, one of the executives said, "So, Janet, how would you market our company?"

That, of course, was, "Tell me about yourself," which would make the meeting about me.

Now, there was no way I was going to answer that question, especially with plate of steaming lasagna in front of me. Instead, I looked at each respective division head in turn and said, "As you know, marketing an apartment property is completely different from marketing an office building, which is totally different from promoting a shopping center, which is completely unlike leasing up an industrial park."

In turn, each division head nodded in agreement. I then steered the conversation back where it belonged – on them, their properties and the company's recent merger with a large real estate concern.

on the West Coast and their desire to pursue third-party property management assignments.

And the next day, the panel informed the CEO that by unanimous vote, I was their new publicist.

CHAPTER THIRTEEN

Handling Questions and Objections

*"I know you believe you understand what you think I said,
but I'm not sure you realize what you heard is not what I meant."*

—Robert McCloskey, Author

TOSS BACK THAT HOT POTATO

"Hell, there are no rules here;
we're trying to accomplish something."

– *Thomas Alva Edison*

S ince this meeting is really about Mr. Bigg and his company, you should not get any Traditional System interrogation-type questions about you. On the contrary, Mr. Bigg should be too focused on himself to focus on you, which is exactly what you want.

Reality Check

Never forget this meeting is *not* about you; it's about Mr. Bigg. If you want to get hired, make sure your meeting is focused completely on him at all times for the duration of the meeting.

If by some remote chance Mr. Bigg does ask you a Traditional System interrogation question, you must respond out of politeness, and here's how you do it:

- First: Acknowledge the question has been asked.
- Second: Don't answer the question.

Instead, shift the conversation back to Mr. Bigg, like this:

Tell me about yourself.
I'd be happy to tell you anything you'd like to know about me. But first, I'd like to know more about your . . .

What is your biggest weakness?
(Smile) Now that's a loaded question. Why don't we discuss the issues you're facing with meeting your deadlines, rather than my fondness for chocolate?

What interests you about our company?
I know you're doing some pretty exciting things with your Whazizit line. How do you plan to roll it out, given the competition's plans to introduce a similar product next spring?

What are your goals over the next five years?
A lot can be accomplished in five years. Do you expect to totally shift your focus to custom fabrication by then?

(Describes problem): How would you handle this?
At the moment, I couldn't tell you because there's a great deal I don't know about the company, its people and the history of the situation. Why don't you bring me up to speed on what's been tried?

Why did you leave your last employer?
Change is a part of life, isn't it? I understand your company is going through some changes right now. What can you tell me about it?

What was your biggest failure?
Every business has challenges, doesn't it? I know your ZamBast line never took off, and we can talk about that another time. I think your MegaMax line is awesome; how are you marketing it to college students?

Why do you want to work for us?
I understand demand for your products is so big you're back-ordered for two months. How can I help you?

What was the last book you read or movie you saw?
I'd love to chat about books or movies, but why don't we save that for a lunch? Right now, I'd like to know how the new bank across the street will affect your marketing plans for next year.

Why should we hire you?
What I find interesting is that your situation has gotten to the point that you can't handle it internally with your current staff. You have some excellent people here and are obviously growing. How can I help you accomplish your goals?

What makes you a good fit for our organization?
You tell me what you're looking for, and I'll tell you if I think we have a match.

To see this technique in action, watch a press conference with any senior-level politician, such as a mayor, senator, governor or president. Notice how they answer questions without answering them, tactfully avoid talking about what they don't want to talk about, and that no one calls them on it.

Talking to Human Resources

If you are forced to visit Human Resources before you are hired by Mr. Bigg, you can fulfill your obligation while completely avoiding being interrogated: just ask the HR person a highly complicated trigger question only Mr. Bigg can answer.

The chances are excellent the HR person won't be able to answer your trigger question unless you are looking for a job in Human Resources (HR professionals see below).

Human Resource professionals are trained in things like governmental compliance, labor relations, employment law, conflict resolution and other employee relations matters. They usually don't know much about the inner workings of other departments.

Reality Check

Since the HR person can't speak for Mr. Bigg or have a peer-to-peer conversation with you about Mr. Bigg's issues, any discussion with

HR is a waste of your time. Remember, Human Resources has no authority to hire you and has no influence over who gets hired.

Let's say you want to work in the occupational health department at a hospital, but first you have to see Human Resources. As the interrogation begins, you say:

> "Last year, your hospital started a weight-loss surgery program and a nutritional weight-loss counseling program that are both now very popular. As a result, you're probably seeing a rise in the number of larger patients throughout the hospital for all kinds of procedures, not just for weight loss.

> "Have you seen an increase in employee injuries with the influx of this patient population since the weight-loss programs began? What procedures have you installed to minimize the possibility of injury to your staff and patients? Do you have a no-lift policy in place?"

Since HR is usually not involved in injury prevention (although they do handle workers' compensation claims) and they know nothing about patient-handling techniques or equipment, they will be clueless, and try to turn the meeting back on you.

Should that happen, gather your things and say, "I see I'm going to have to talk to Mr. Bigg about this after all. Thanks, anyway." Then leave.

Although the meeting was a total waste of your time, you have fulfilled your obligation to meet with HR, and are now totally free to meet with the Director of Occupational Health.

Reality Check for HR Professionals

The only person you should meet with is the Director of Human Resources or another senior-level line person, such as the President or Chief Financial Officer, who understands that the true function of Human Resources is to maximize the value of the company's biggest asset – its employees.

Reject Rejection

Uh-oh. You know what the letter says even before you open the envelope or email:

> "Thank you for contacting our company, and we regret that we are unable to offer you the position you seek at this time. We appreciate your interest, and we wish you every success in your future endeavors."

The bad news about asking for something is that if you ask enough people or the same people enough times, most of them will eventually say "no."

The good news about asking for something is that if you ask enough people or the same people enough times, most of them will eventually say "yes."

And the best news of all is that when you're looking for a job, all you need is one person to say "yes" once.

Reality Check

Rejection does not exist in business because business is all about transactions, usually involving money.

Everyone has been rejected some time:

♦ You got stood up for a date.

♦ The person you're trying to date never calls you, returns your calls, emails you or responds to your emails.

♦ Your partner told you the relationship was over, or your partner never said the words but treated you like the relationship was over.

♦ The person you are trying to have a relationship with won't see you, is never home and is dating someone else.

♦ The person you thought you had a relationship with moved

without telling you that he moved, when he moved, where he moved to or how to reach him. Three weeks later, he calls saying he's been "busy."

Despite your best efforts, you will probably get a few negative responses during your job search. After all, not everyone needs you right now or is smart enough to realize how great it would be to have you working for them, and they're entitled to be wrong.

I Said No!

You say "no" all the time in one way or another:

> "I'm too tired."
> "Take me off your email list."
> "I'm not interested."
> "That's not right."
> "I'm just looking."
> "No, thanks."

When you say "no" to other people, do they cringe, hide in the corner, give up trying because it's pointless to go on, or claim they're no good? No? Well, why should you?

Think back. There was a time when "no" didn't bother you a bit. In fact, you knew that each "no" got you closer to the "yes" you wanted, so you relished receiving them:

You (as a kid): "Can I have a cookie, please?"

Mom (acting parental): "No, it will spoil your dinner."

You (calling her bluff): "It won't, I'll eat everything."

Mom (she's heard that line before): "No, it's too close to dinner time."

You (determined to win): "But I'm really hungry now!"

Mom (weakening): "One cookie, but you have to eat all your vegetables."

You (going for the kill): "Even the beans? Ewww."

Mom (caving): "I'll give you a half portion of beans, but you must eat all of them."

You (knowing a good deal): "Okay."

Mom (handing you the cookie): "You'd better eat every one of those beans."

In triumph, you take the cookie and go watch TV until dinner. Boy, you're good; you not only got that cookie, but you scored a bonus: tonight you only have to eat a half portion of those icky beans.

You got what you wanted and more because you refused to hear "no." You knew if you were persistent enough, Mom would give in and even if she didn't, you could always try again tomorrow.

But as you grew up, you not only began to hear "no," you started to take it personally. And now when you get a "no" for reasons that have nothing to do with you, it's like a door has been slammed in your face, and all you want to do is go back to bed.

Objection Overruled

Here's a tip from a professional salesperson: if you are talking to the right person about their needs, interests and concerns, nearly all of the time, a "no" is a "yes" in disguise; these are called "objections."

Rather than being obstacles, objections are actually buying signals because Mr. Bigg *has* to be interested in you in order to have objections!

If you are focusing the meeting on Mr. Bigg, any "no" you get most likely means, "Not now," or "I don't have enough information," or "I don't have enough of the right information." It never means, "Go away; we hate you and don't ever come back."

Traditional System objections are almost asked exclusively by HR as part of their interrogation tactics. Since you are not meeting with HR or allowing yourself to be interrogated, you never have to worry about them.

However, old beliefs die hard, and you may be concerned you'll get such Traditional System objections as:

- You're overqualified for this job.
- You don't have enough experience.
- You seem to be a job hopper.
- You've been out of work a long time.
- You don't have the background we're looking for.
- You'll probably leave us after a little while.

The Traditional System's numerous techniques for handling such objections include putting you on the defensive, making you justify why you aren't overqualified, and forcing you to explain how the experience you have is good enough for them.

You have to describe how your skills transfer over; how you've made productive use of your "extended vacation," how you are happy in a variety of work environments, and that you're looking forward to contributing to the company's long-term success.

But no matter what you say, the best you can hope for is to neutralize their overt implication you're not what they want. Because you're on the defensive, you don't feel you said the right thing, and you'll never know if you did.

Reality Check

Mr. Bigg should be too busy talking about himself to raise issues that will prevent him from hiring you. In fact, he will do everything he can to convince himself he has to hire you.

Mr. Bigg will probably have questions or concerns, but these are just to get the two of you in sync so you can cut a deal beneficial to you both. Just remember: he's talking to you *because* he's interested in you!

Say, What?

Here is a very effective way to handle Traditional System objections, especially any given by an HR person. Rather than immediately responding, pause, take a deep breath, smile, and ask the HR person to clarify his objection. What you're hearing may be completely different from what he's saying, and his objection is probably irrelevant anyway.

Let's say the Human Resources person says, "You don't have the kind of experience we're looking for." The "qualifications/experience" issue is one of the most common Traditional System objections, but is utterly ridiculous when you think about it.

If a company wants an MBA with ten years of experience in international corporate finance, and you have a B.A. in accounting and three years experience at a local savings bank, why did they ask to see you? Have they nothing better to do than interview unqualified applicants?

According to the Traditional System, only the most likely candidates make it to the interview stage. So, you got the meeting because you are qualified and because they believe you can do the job! If they didn't believe that, they wouldn't be wasting their time talking to you.

Reality Check

To respond to a Traditional System objection, just turn the statement into a question; if you are asked a question, reply with a question. Do not answer, address or acknowledge the objection has any validity whatsoever; it doesn't.

Here is how you handle the "lack of experience" objection:

You don't have the kind of experience we want.
What kind of experience do you want?

Rather than you having to explain why you're wasting the HR person's time when you don't have what they want, now they have to explain why they're wasting your time when they knew all along you didn't have what they wanted.

Here are more Contrarian answers to Traditional System interview questions (see Chapter 14 for money questions):

You're overqualified for this job.
What do you mean, "overqualified"?

You don't have enough experience.
Define "enough."

Why did you leave your last job?
Haven't you ever broken up with anyone?

Why were you fired from your last job?
Haven't you ever had someone break up with you?

You probably won't be happy here.
What makes people happy here?

Why have you stayed so long at that company?
Doesn't this company value loyalty in its employees?

Why haven't you found a job yet?
Why haven't you filled this job yet?

Why haven't you ever been promoted?
Why aren't you promoting someone from the inside?

Does your employer know that you're looking?
Do your employees know that you're looking?

Have you ever been arrested or convicted?
Do you hire ex-cons?

We don't have many employees here who are your age.
Would that bother you?
Would it bother you if many of your employees were my age?

What do you think of your ex-boss?
What do you think of your ex-employees?

How have you helped reduce costs?
Does this company value quantity over quality?

Military people are too rigid. We operate in a fluid, action-packed environment.
Have you ever been on a battlefield?

We need someone with agency experience.
How is that important when this is an in-house job?

We're looking for someone with five years experience.
How did you arrive at the number "five"?

What types of problems do you struggle with?
What types of problems are causing the company to struggle?

Why should we hire you?
Why would I want to work here?

Why do you want this job?
Why do you need someone to do this job?

Explain those gaps in your resume.
Haven't you ever done anything in your life besides work?

Are you talking to other companies at this time?
Are you talking to other applicants at this time?

You're not qualified for this job.
Then why are we talking?

The Unspoken Objection

Even if you are meeting with Mr. Bigg and the meeting is going great, there may be an unspoken objection you can sense but is never addressed. This happened in my last dip back into the corporate world in 2000.

Since leaving commercial real estate, I had spent four years selling mobility and rehab products. After having worked for two deal-ers, I decided my next step was to be a corporate sales representative in Texas for a manufacturer or distributor of rehab products.

One of the five companies that met my criteria was Otto Bock HealthCare, a global prosthetics manufacturer who had an excellent reputation for its wheelchair accessories and positioning products. I called the company's US headquarters in Minneapolis and asked, "Who is your sales manager for Texas?"

The customer service gal said, "Our Southern Regional Sales Manager is 'Eric' _____. His extension is 1138. Let me give you his voice mail."

Simply by making one brief phone call, I had Mr. Bigg's name, title and extension number and had left him a voice mail telling him who I was, what I did and that I'd like to sell his products. I had no idea if Otto Bock needed a rehab sales rep in Texas, but I certainly had nothing to lose by asking.

Eric returned my call the next day. He said it was interesting I called because they were now looking for a rehab sales rep for Texas and Oklahoma.

Somehow, I was not surprised that, once again, I was in the right place at the right time. Since this opportunity had come to me as easily and effortlessly as all my other jobs, I knew, with absolutely certainty, that this job was already mine.

I then snail mailed Eric a letter, my resume and a pamphlet I had written for consumers on Medicare coverage of scooters when I sold mobility products. I could have emailed these items, but I wanted Eric to hold the pamphlet so he would see it as consumers saw it.

One week later and the day he received my materials, Eric called me. He was not supposed to call me; I was supposed to call him. By calling me, Eric had tipped his hand – he was clearly very interested in me and I knew it. He was buying.

Eric asked if I could I meet him at the airport in a few weeks; we'd talk over lunch since he was going to meet the two other can-didates – both of whom were rehab seating specialists – in separate meetings that day.

By then, I had four years experience in mobility and rehab sales, but I had never evaluated a client for equipment, fitted a client in a wheelchair or customized a seating system, and these two guys did that for a living.

Theoretically, these rehab specialists were in sales, but based upon my experience at the rehab dealership, I knew they simply worked whatever business came in through referrals.

They assessed the patients and their environments, determined what equipment was needed, had their office get the paperwork from the clinicians and the funding approved, and then they ordered and delivered the equipment.

This was not selling; this was an elaborate form of order taking. If these two guys were typical rehab technicians like ones I had worked with, it was a sure bet they did not sell proactively and had no training, education or experience in corporate selling or business development.

I doubted if Eric even knew what a rehab seating specialist did, much less how they "sold." My suspicions were confirmed when Eric said he didn't know anything about rehab because he came from the prosthetics side of the business.

Over lunch at the airport, Eric and I discussed the company's rehab products; I had printed out pages about the company's wheelchairs from its website and talked about each one. Eric was fascinated but obviously lost.

And that was the problem. It would be a natural decision for Eric – a top prosthetics salesperson recently promoted to regional sales manager who knew nothing about rehab – to hire a certified, experienced, rehab specialist to sell his rehab products.

I realized, but clearly Eric did not, that this was a *sales* job. The products happened to be rehab products, but the buyers were therapists at hospitals and rehab dealers, not patients.

The Otto Bock sales rep would never see patients, fit them in a wheelchair or evaluate them for a seating system, so experience working with clients and professional credentials didn't matter.

What was needed for this job was someone with sales experience, a well-rounded background in rehab products, and a basic understanding of physical disabilities so the sales rep could talk intelligently to the clinicians and dealers who were dealing directly with the patients. This I had.

Clearly, Eric's unspoken objection to me was that I did not have hands-on experience with patients or the credentials the other candidates had. But I knew this objection was bogus because this was a sales job, not a clinical job, and clinical credentials were irrelevant; I just had to make him realize it.

So, as the meeting ended, I told Eric I had one final question for him:

Janet: "How did the other two guys find you?"

Eric: "They heard through the grapevine that we were looking for a sales rep and they contacted me." Pausing and looking hard at me, he said, "How did *you* find me?"

Janet: "I picked up the phone. I spoke to you."

Eric: "Yes, but how did you know we were hiring?"

Janet: "I didn't. I was prospecting." (Prospecting is the first step in selling; being a professional salesperson, Eric would instinctively know this.)

Eric, looking confused and then getting it: "Ahhh!"

It took him a few seconds, but he got my point: what kind of a sales rep did he want on his sales force – someone who is passive, reactive and only takes action when they hear of an opportunity, or someone who is assertive, proactive and *finds* opportunities?

Eric said he would be tied up in a meeting the next day, but I would hear from him at 10:30 a.m. the day after. Two days later at 10:30 a.m., it's Eric on the phone saying those magic words:

"How would you like to work for us?"

CHAPTER FOURTEEN

Getting the Money and the "Yes"

"I don't know the key to success,
but the key to failure is trying to please everybody."

—Bill Cosby, Comedian

SHOW ME THE MONEY

"Why is there so much month left at the end of the money?"

– John Barrymore

Traditional System interview interrogation money questions usually deal with your financial history and generally probe how much you're willing to give up in order to get hired:

- What do you think you are worth?
- What were you paid in your last job?
- Why aren't you earning more at your age?
- Would you be willing to take a pay cut?
- How important is money to you?
- What is the minimum salary you will accept?
- What would you like to earn in five years?
- What was the most you ever made in a year?

Reality Check

Never discuss your current or past compensation history, financial situation or monetary goals with anyone in a job interview. This information is personal, private, irrelevant to the meeting, and is none of their business.

The issue of money is definitely important, but make sure it is Mr. Bigg who talks about money first because when he talks money, it means he is buying and he is buying you. The question is usually, "What kind of salary do you want?"

The best way to answer this question is not to answer it. Say that you'd rather discuss money later, and turn the conversation back to being about Mr. Bigg and/or his company. Regardless of the topic you discuss, just make sure you're not it.

Under no circumstances should you ever volunteer a number – you'll lose no matter what you say because you don't know what his "acceptable" level is. If you're over that arbitrary number, you're automatically out, and if you're under, you'll be underpaid and he'll know it, but you won't.

Do your homework on typical salary ranges at sites like www. salary.com, and then shoot for the top of the range, especially if you think you don't have a chance of getting it. You'll never know how much you could get if you don't ask for it.

Conversely, never accept anything below your preset minimum, and be ready to walk if you can't strike a deal you'll be happy with. That's precisely what Mr. Bigg would do.

Toss 'Em Some Coins

Regardless of the amount of money you plan to ask for, Mr. Bigg will probably object to it. This is only human nature: why should he pay more for something if he could get away with paying less?

Reality Check

Any objection you get about money is probably false.

Chances are you only want a few thousand dollars more than Mr. Bigg says they can afford, but don't you believe it. Aren't the lights on? Aren't there people walking around? Aren't the phones ringing? Isn't this company making money?

Do you really believe those few thousand dollars are going to push that company into bankruptcy? Would you want to work for a company that's so close to the brink of financial disaster?

No? Well, think about this: the guy sitting across from you telling you they can't afford you is making at least three to five times what you say you want, and he's not hurting. So they *have* the money. The issue then is not the money; the issue is getting them to spend the money on you.

You Want How Much?

When was the last time you paid more than you should have for something, but you didn't mind because you thought you were getting a bargain or you wanted it right then?

Ignoring the price tag when you want something is the difference between cost and value." "Cost" is what something is worth to other people at any time; "value" is what something is worth to you right now.

Reality Check

The whole point of the Contrarian System is to get Mr. Bigg to want you, because when he wants you, he will meet your price.

A great example of cost vs. value is in the movie "Jerry Maguire." Jerry is a sports agent who gets fired and loses all of his clients except one – a short, lightweight, pompous football player who thinks he's God's gift to the game.

He tells Jerry to get him a $10 million, multi-year contract with his current team, Arizona, because his contract is about to expire and he doesn't want to become a free agent.

The Arizona team owner tells Jerry that the football player isn't worth the $1.1 million he's now getting, and what's more, he'll be dropped from the team when his contract expires.

Fast forward the movie to the Super Bowl finals game with Arizona needing one touchdown to win. As the clock ticks away the last few minutes of the game, the football player does an incredible, impossible leap to catch the ball, flips and lands on his back, knocking himself unconscious.

The doctors rush to the field and the crowd is on its feet; even the television reporters speak in hushed tones. It's a first: Arizona is going to the Super Bowl, but nobody cares.

And then, miraculously, the football player wakes up unhurt. Lying on the ground hidden from view by the doctors, he realizes he is the newest star of Big League football and springs to his feet, celebrating his victory along with millions of cheering fans.

His payoff is a four-year contract with Arizona worth $11.2 million. The Arizona team owner is now happy to be paying ten times what he was paying before for the exact same football player. But nothing about the football player has changed; he's still short, lightweight, mediocre, and now even more pompous than he was at the beginning of the movie.

The only thing that has changed is in the eyes of the team own, the football player's value as a contributing member of the team has skyrocketed. Before the game, the team owner had thought only in terms of the football player's cost to him.

But with the football player now the MVP who took his team to the Super Bowl, you can imagine the team owner is thinking: "I now have the hottest player in the league and his contract is just about up. If he becomes a free agent, he'll be worth at least $15 million, so I'll low-ball him at $11 million and see what happens."

What happens is that everyone wins. The football player gets his $10 million and a new contract with the team of his choice, Jerry gets a cool $1 million commission, is instantly the hottest agent in sports, and the team owner gets his prized player – at a discount!

We're In The Money

In the Traditional System, you're supposed to defend your position, justify your reasoning and explain why you have the audacity to believe you are worth the money you are requesting, like this:

> Your salary range is too high.
> *My experience and training make me ideal to handle this position, and I am well worth what I am asking. In my last position, my programs saved my employer . .*

Since you know any money objection Mr. Bigg gives you is false, all you have to do is make him prove it.

Reality Check
Handle money objections like any other objection – just turn the statement or question into a question. Do not answer, respond or validate it in any way.

A common money objection is the amount you want:

> Your salary range is too high.
> *What do you mean, "too high?"*

All you need to do now is just sit there silently and wait for Mr. Bigg to respond. Don't say a word; just allow the pressure of the silence to do its work.

When Mr. Bigg finally speaks, he will attempt to defend his reasons for trying to not pay you fairly, explain how his company can't afford you (even though it can afford him quite comfortably) or justify the company's rigid compensation structure, which he neglected to mention before and from which he is exempt.

Then you two can discuss what Mr. Bigg expects to receive for the money he's going to pay you, and at that point, you can decide whether it's worth your time to continue the discussion.

Here are more Contrarian System answers to Traditional System money questions and objections:

> What kind of salary do you want?
> *What kind of compensation package are you offering?*

> What did you make on your last job?
> *How is that relevant to this job with your company?*

> You're asking too much money.
> *How much do you think good talent is worth?*

> We need to run a credit check on you before you can get hired.
> *Since this position does not involve money, finance or investments, why is that important?*

Would you be willing to take a pay cut for the right opportunity with our company?
How can any opportunity with this company be "right" if you don't compensate your employees competitively?

We're speaking to other candidates who are willing to accept less than you are to work here.
If you were offered a job with this company that paid less for the same work than you could get at another firm, would you take it?

Whatever they tell you, don't buy their excuses. If the company really can't afford you, you can't afford to work there. This is not the only company on the planet and is not the only place at which you should consider working.

Reality Check

If you believe there is a salary cap you cannot breach, aren't worth or don't deserve, you're right. But if you believe you are worth a certain amount of money or more, so will the people you are talking to.

When it comes to negotiating, don't ever be afraid to ask for what you want, even if you think you're making an outlandish request. It may not seem outlandish to Mr. Bigg at all.

The worst that can happen is you get a "no" to some items, but you know Mr. Bigg wants you (if he didn't, he wouldn't be negotiating with you), and deals are rarely lost over minor points.

You're not being greedy or selfish when you ask for what you want, and Mr. Bigg knows this; you just want to be fairly compensated for what you're going to contribute to his company. After all, he is.

The Extra Edge

If you really want Mr. Bigg to think "Wow!" about you, you have to do more than just show up and have a great meeting that is focused on him. The key is to act as if you are already an employee by bringing something to the meeting that shows it:

- A would-be sales rep for a natural food chain developed a menu using ingredients from their stores. The executives hired her while they were munching.

- A teacher developed a sample curriculum and gave a mini-lesson in a subject she wanted to introduce to the school.

- Knowing an architectural firm was about to do work on renovating a downtown eyesore, a junior architect researched the building's history and sketched some ideas.

- A would-be copywriter developed a marketing campaign for a make-believe product similar to those represented by the agency she wanted to work for.

Because this is something you have done on your own initiative, Mr. Bigg will realize how terrific you are without your having to say it.

Don't Call Us, We'll Call You

But should Mr. Bigg hand you a report and ask for your feedback or ask you to do any kind of work for free, alarm bells should be ringing loudly in your mind.

Providing a free sample of your work is called "auditioning," but unless you're going to a casting call, don't even consider it. If you are ever asked to work for free as a condition of getting hired, pause, look calmly at the person making this outlandish request and say quietly:

> "I'd be happy to do this assignment for you. My consulting rate is $_____ an hour or I can estimate a flat fee. Would you like me to prepare a proposal?"

Then say nothing. You have now tactfully forced Mr. Bigg to tell you exactly where you stand with him. Chances are that you will either get the job to do the work or you'll do the work and get a consulting fee.

If Mr. Bigg tells you he won't hire you without you doing the work for free, tell him you're sure he'll find someone suitable for the position and then leave.

Don't be surprised if you get a phone call asking you to reconsider, but think twice about accepting a job there. If he has so little regard for you as a candidate, imagine how he'll treat you as an employee.

Reality Check

Never agree or volunteer to do work for free that you would otherwise be paid for. You will undervalue yourself, show how desperate you are to get hired, and make Mr. Bigg lose whatever respect he had for you.

Think about it: why would Mr. Bigg want to hire someone who thinks so little of themselves that they give away their work just for the asking? He wouldn't.

I Want To Work Here

Being in front of Mr. Bigg and listening to him talk isn't enough to get you hired. You must literally ask for the job because it will not be given to you unless you do.

Unfortunately, the Traditional System teaches you to use aggressive, overt and pushy hard-sell tactics designed to manipulate Mr. Bigg into a "yes" like this:

"From everything we've discussed, it seems like I am an excellent fit for this position. Do you agree?"

"I know I can meet the demands of the position and would make an outstanding contribution. When can I start?"

"Your search is now over. You will not find anyone else more qualified to do this job than me. If I were you, I'd cancel all the other interviews and make me an offer right now."

Did you count the "I's" and "you's" in these questions? Did you notice how they're all about the person who wants to get hired, and not the person doing the hiring?

Reality Check

You got the meeting because Mr. Bigg believes you can help him, and you can tell from the way he treats you how eager he is to have you working for him.

So stop trying to make it happen; relax and allow Mr. Bigg the pleasure of hiring you.

Oh, Wow!

Instead of manipulation, try honesty. If you are really interested in working for Mr. Bigg and that company, say so!

Reality Check

Because he can't read your mind, you have to tell Mr. Bigg if you're as enthused about working for him as he is having you work for him.

If you are, it should be easy for you to make several strong, honest expressions of interest to let Mr. Bigg know in no uncertain terms that you want to work for him, like this:

"This is a terrific challenge, and I'd like to show you what I can do with it."

"What a great company this must be to work for!"

"You said this particular project has top priority? I'd want to focus on that first."

"After talking with you, I'm not surprised your turnover is so low. No wonder my friends love it here."

"I had no idea of the depth of your services. This firm must be one of the best kept secrets in the business."

Once you have made an expression of interest, expect Mr. Bigg to stare or maybe smile at you, but to say nothing. He will probably be so shocked at your genuine enthusiasm he won't know what to say. Don't mind him; you just keep on admiring his wonderful company, and pretty soon, Mr. Bigg will think you're pretty wonderful too.

Am I In or What?

One great nonverbal sign that you have been hired or are a very serious candidate is when Mr. Bigg starts handing you things, such as a company newsletter or brochures. If he hands you a company directory, you have been hired, whether or not the words are actually spoken.

But if Mr. Bigg hasn't already given you the nod one way or another, you have to know where you stand with him, and it's very easy to find out. Toward the end of the meeting, just ask him, "So, what do you think?" and wait for him to respond. What he will tell you will be the truth and most likely will be in your favor.

This Stuff Works #4

Shortly after my experience with the public relations agency, I got an interview with the chairman of the board of Landauer Associates, the big commercial real estate consulting firm.

Landauer specialized in unique projects few companies could touch, such as appraising the value of Rockefeller Center and advising General Motors on the location of the yet-to-be-built Saturn manufacturing facility.

This was pretty exciting stuff in commercial real estate, and I really wanted to be a part of it. Landauer had five offices across the country and had its headquarters in New York, where it was essentially run by "John," its chairman and second CEO in the company's 40-year history.

John, who had been with Landauer for decades, was a living legend in commercial real estate, and I was going to meet him. In our meeting, John and I sat catty-corner to each other on adjacent couches; this was ideal because I could gauge his physical responses to whatever I said up close.

Knowing his long history with the company, I figured that

Landauer was the center of John's life and noticed that every time I said the word "Landauer," John would unconsciously nod and his eyes would dilate slightly.

So, I talked about what was best for *Landauer*, how *Landauer* would benefit from improving its visibility in the press, how writing about *Landauer* would be a joy, and how *Landauer* had a great reputation, but was relatively unknown outside the industry, etc.

With every *Landauer*, John would nod and his eyes would dilate, but at times he was strangely distant and would briefly go blank.

Much later, when his behavior became so erratic and unpredictable that he had to be eased out of the company, I realized that at the time of our meeting, John had been in the early stages of Alzheimer's disease.

Whenever John would blank out, I would pull him back into awareness by either saying something he didn't expect or by emphasizing Landauer strongly. One of the things I said that brought him back was, "I am so thrilled to be here. Landauer is the ultimate real estate consulting firm."

Every time I made an expression of interest, John simply looked at me and said nothing, and I would continue the conversation. Three days later, the job was mine.

I later learned that I had beaten out 250 people who had responded to a blind ad placed just once in the Sunday New York Times (the internet did not exist then). Of course I hadn't seen the ad, since I never read the want ads when I was looking for a job.

The job actually came to me through a relay of referrals – one real estate advertising agency in Manhattan would steer me to six others. This was not networking in the Traditional System sense because I didn't know anyone at these agencies nor did I have a target company in mind; I was just open to whatever possibilities these referrals would generate.

It took a month of these referrals for me to connect with Art, the president of New York's biggest commercial real estate advertising agency. I sent Art my resume and writing samples, and when I called him a week later, he said, "I have nothing here, but I'd like to talk with you about something somewhere else. Can you come down tomorrow?"

Unknown to me, one of Art's clients was Landauer, and Landauer was looking for an in-house public relations person. Art was a commercial real estate publicist from way back, and he now was recruiting and screening public relations candidates for Landauer.

I could not have timed it better had I tried. Art received my material the Wednesday before the ad ran in the Sunday paper, and I met with him the Wednesday after the ad ran, and before the resumes would begin to pour in from applicants.

After we settled in, Art showed me the ad. It didn't just have my name on it; it was screaming, "Janet, where have you been?" This was everything I possibly could have wanted in a job as a commercial real estate writer and publicist.

I didn't even know this job existed, and now it was literally being handed to me. But it was a blind ad – who could the company be? As I silently read the ad, Art smiled and said, "The company is Landauer." Of course I knew who Landauer was, and I instantly knew this was the job of my dreams.

Keeping totally calm and nonchalant, I looked up briefly and simply said, "Oh." But inside I was thinking, "Landauer needs a writer? THIS JOB IS MINE!"

And Art said, "You not only have everything we're looking for; you exceed it." He then picked up the phone and called "Jim," Landauer's executive vice president and my potential boss, saying: "I have a candidate for the public relations position. Can we come down tomorrow?"

You read it right; he said "we." This seasoned veteran of big league New York City commercial real estate marketing, public relations and advertising was not just recommending me for the job; he was endorsing me.

The next day, Art and I met with Jim, who was cordial but noncommittal. I later learned Jim preferred another candidate named "Pat," but he was outvoted by John and Landauer's president and vice chairman, who I did not meet, but both of whom had read my materials and knew a commercial real estate person when they saw one.

Pat had great public relations agency credentials in retail banking, but she had no training or experience in commercial real estate.

She was going for a job in an industry where she didn't know the business, couldn't speak the language, didn't know who was who, how things worked or why things were the way they were.

I had no formal public relations experience and had never worked in an agency, but had been in commercial real estate for six years, had a Master's degree in Urban Planning from New York University, and was an accomplished commercial real estate writer with the clippings to prove it.

Logically, the three senior industry veterans at this real estate company would be inclined to go with me because I could hit the ground writing, despite Jim's preference for Pat. And that's just what they did.

At the staff meeting held a week after I started, John put his arm around my shoulder and formally introduced me:

"Everybody, I want you to meet Janet White, our new Director of Public Relations. I'm so happy she's with us because she really wanted to work here."

Yes, I really did.

CHAPTER FIFTEEN

The Encore

"Do or do not. There is no try."

—Yoda in "Star Wars: The Empire Strikes Back"

JUST ONE MORE THING . . .

"I know nothing stays the same,
but if you're willing to play the game,
it's coming around again."

– Carly Simon

Perhaps the most misused and misunderstood tool of the Traditional System is the "thank-you note." Careerjournal.com has this to say about it: "Hiring managers agree that a topnotch thank-you letter must include the following components:

♦ An opening paragraph in which you express your appreciation for the interview.

♦ A second paragraph that reinforces your understanding of the position's requirements and emphasizes your qualifications. Be sure to include any important information about yourself that you may have omitted during the interview.

♦ If necessary, a third paragraph to correct any misunderstanding the interviewer might have following your meeting. You can also use this paragraph to counter an objection the interviewer raised about an aspect of your background.

◆ A final paragraph that expresses your interest in the position and the company."

The Traditional System insists you must send a thank-you note within 24 hours to Mr. Bigg and everyone else you meet during your visit to that company, especially if the interview didn't go well, the vibes weren't right or the job you thought you were going for turned out to be something else.

Reality Check

If a company isn't a match for you, don't bother following up on the meeting; it's a waste of your time and theirs.

After a bad blind date, would you contact the other person to make it all better or because you were "supposed to"? If you wouldn't do this in your personal life, don't do it in your professional life.

According to the Traditional System, writing a thank-you note supposedly will make Mr. Bigg remember you, get him to change his mind about you so he'll hire you, or at least pass your name along to other people who could hire you. Don't bet on it.

Love Me Do

Here are some Traditional System thank-you notes; each has "I vs. you" scores and comments:

To Emphasize "Fit" With the Company

Thank you for taking the time to discuss the insurance broker position at California Investments with me. After meeting with you and observing the company's operations, I am further convinced that my background and skills coincide well with your needs.

I really appreciate that you took so much time to acquaint me with the company. It is no wonder that California Investments retains its employees for so long. I feel I could learn a great deal from you and would certainly enjoy working with you.

Along with my unique qualifications and specialized experience, I bring excellent work habits and judgment to this position. With the countless demands on your time, I am sure that you require people who can be trusted to carry out their responsibilities with minimal supervision.

I look forward to hearing from you concerning your hiring decision. Again, thank you for your time and consideration.

Score: I's: 11 You's: 14

Comments: This letter has more you's than I's, but it is clearly all about the applicant, not Mr. Bigg. The applicant never once mentions what Mr. Bigg discussed in their meeting or anything about what the company does. Too bad; he probably was a viable candidate, but his "thank-you note" eliminated him from consideration.

Damage Control After A "Bad" Interview

Thank you for the time you took to interview me for the seminar leader position. After our interview, I'm convinced that I have the three ingredients you're looking for in your workshop/seminar leaders.

I know you expressed some concern in our meeting that I have not worked in a personnel department. I want to stress that I have participated significantly in the hiring process for my sorority and have a solid record of achievement in my Human Resources classes.

As for your requirement for public-speaking experience, I led new-student orientation groups at my college for three years, and received outstanding grades in my public speaking classes, which qualifies me nicely. I have enclosed several writing samples to demonstrate the third ingredient, my communications skills.

Thank you again for this wonderful opportunity to interview for the seminar leader position. I promise you I won't let you down if you give me the chance to show what I can do. I eagerly await the next step in the process.

Score: I's: 18 You's: 10

Comments: This may indeed be a wonderful opportunity for some new grad, but not this candidate. She obviously didn't have what the company wanted, which raises the question of why she got the meeting at all.

However, it was good practice for her; perhaps someday she'll realize her collegiate activities and class assignments don't count as professional experience, and that groveling will never get her hired.

To Provide Additional Information

I'd like to thank you for the time you spent talking with me about the marketing research analyst position you have open at Razzle magazine. I am excited about this position and convinced that my training equips me more than adequately for the job.

I meant to mention that last summer I attended a three-week intensive seminar on SPSS, the foremost marketing-research software package. I know the job description mentions the ability to use SPSS, and I wanted to make sure you knew I am extremely well-versed in the use of this software.

Please contact me if you have any questions about my ability with this program or about any of my other qualifications. As you know, my work-study position in the institutional research office here at Rutgers provided an excellent background for marketing research.

I look forward to hearing from you soon about the position, and I again thank you for meeting with me.

Score: I's: 17 You's: 9

Comments: Clearly, knowledge of this special software program was a key component of the job, but if they didn't discuss this in the interview, what *did* they talk about?

Like so many Traditional System thank-you notes, this one attempts to "make right" a meeting in which the applicant was left with the sinking feeling he wasn't going to get the job.

To Entice The Employer

I want to thank you for taking the time to interview me yesterday for the position of assistant director of the Dayton Sumner Memorial Art Museum.

You, Mr. Dawson, and Dr. Acquino exuded warmth, and I know we could all have an excellent working relationship. As I further studied the job description for the position, I grew even more confident that I could take the museum to new heights of success.

With the resources I've gathered, I can hit the ground running with grant writing. The 15% bonus is an excellent incentive, and I will devote a significant portion of my time to this important venture.

I also have a number of great ideas for community and media relations, and am excited by your interest in bringing more schoolchildren to the museum.

As I mentioned when we met, I would like to use my fine arts degree and journalism minor to enhance the museum's identity, while meeting the needs and expectations of the community.

I believe I can make a significant contribution to the fundraising effort, and I am particularly interested in exploring a corporate donor program.

I am convinced I could bring a new degree of organization to the museum, including sinking my teeth into making the workspace far less chaotic and far more functional.

More importantly, I'd like to get communications on track so that newsletters and invitations are sent out on a timely basis. I have some ideas for making the newsletter more user-friendly. I feel it is extremely important to maintain close communication between the board and directors, and I am committed to doing so.

Thank you again for considering me for this position. I look forward to the possibility of working with you.

Score: I's: 26 You's: 8

Comments: The issues raised in this letter were clearly discussed in the interview, but why did the applicant wait until now to say she has "some ideas" about them?

She could have been hired right in the meeting by discussing her ideas with the very people who would be involved with implementing them. Instead, she leaves open the possibility she won't be hired.

Also, her reference to the 15% bonus for bringing in grants comes across rather tactlessly. She seems more interested in the commission she'd make, rather than what the grants could do for the museum.

Sadly, she ended her letter weakly, indicating she's not the doer she makes herself out to be. Her statement, "I look forward to the possibility of working with you" really says:

"I've got you believing I take the initiative, do the necessary follow-through and can get things done. I do have great ideas; seeing them through is another story.

"What you don't yet know is that I usually leave things open-ended and unfinished, expecting other people to pick up the slack. So if you want to hire me, it's all up to you now."

Her credentials and enthusiasm make her a very strong candidate, but her "thank-you note" neutralizes the great impression she made at the interview. And that's a pity because this could easily have been a slam-dunk.

Ask Not What Your Employer Can Do For You

I appreciate the time you gave me yesterday afternoon. I felt our meeting was as enjoyable as it was informative. After thinking about your Regional Sales Manager position and the goals set for it by the home office, I'm confident that I would be able to meet and exceed those numbers.

As we discussed, I've had extensive experience building both distributor networks and direct-sales organizations in the specialty chemicals industry as well as in others.

My record has been stellar, with numerous awards and bonuses for outstanding increases in revenues and new accounts, plus the recruiting, training and development of talented and promotable sales personnel.

I consider your Regional Sales Manager position to be consistent with my plans for growth. Additionally, your company is a leader in the industry, with an outstanding reputation for rewarding top producers. In short, I think the job would be an excellent career move for me.

Thanks again for the meeting, and I look forward to hearing from you.

Score: I's: 12 You's: 5

Comments: Salespeople never die; they just keep trying to close. Here he is in the final stages of making this sale, yet he's still hammering away at his "prospect" with his qualifications. Whoops! His insecurities are showing.

The major problem with this letter is that this applicant has either forgotten or ignored the fact that Mr. Bigg is a human being who is the center of his own universe and has his own priorities.

As such, Mr. Bigg has no interest in how this job could further the applicant's career or how much money the applicant could make. Mr. Bigg is only interested in furthering his own career by boosting his division's bottom line so that everyone in the company can benefit from the work of its top producers.

And unfortunately, this is what Careerjournal.com calls "an effective thank-you note."

No Thanks

A Traditional System thank-you note is like a Traditional System cover letter – it's all about the person who is writing it, not the person who is reading it, and it usually backfires.

Of course you should always express gratitude when someone does you a favor, gives you a gift, or gives of themselves to you in some way. But Mr. Bigg did not do you a favor by meeting you; he was simply conducting business.

By thanking Mr. Bigg for seeing you, you place him in a position of power and authority over you, and rather than showcasing your unity with each other, you emphasize how far apart you believe you really are from him.

Reality Check

You want Mr. Bigg to see you as a colleague already on the payroll, which is how you should be seeing yourself all along.

If your thank-you note implies you are at the mercy of Mr. Bigg's whim, then you believe you are really helpless and powerless when it comes to getting hired. And the Law of Attraction will make sure you get plenty of demonstrations proving just how helpless and powerless you really are.

Thank You, Thank You, Thank You

But what do you do if you've had a panel interview, or met with several Mr. Biggs one after another? The Traditional System tells you to send a different thank you note to each person or send one thank-you note to a key person for distribution to the others.

Well, the Traditional System has it half right. Panel interviews can be intimidating, simply because you're not having a conversation with several people one at a time; you're being interrogated by them as a group.

Should you choose to contact panel members after your meeting, you don't need to vary your letters to each one; just email the leader and copy the others, or email all of them together as a group. After all, that's how they met you.

If you meet with different people in different departments on a one-on-one basis, remember that they each have different perspectives on how you'll help them accomplish their goals. As a result, you will be writing something different to each person.

This should not be difficult if you treated each one as an individual Mr. Bigg and took notes as they talked. All you have to do now is feed back to them just what they told you, and they'll think you're brilliant because you're thinking just like they do.

Here's What You Think

In business, proposals are used when one company wants to hire another. A typical proposal includes:

◆ A summary of the client's situation as he told it to you.
◆ A strategy for addressing the situation describing how your solutions or suggestions will be developed and delivered.
◆ Biographies of the people doing the work and/or executives of the company.
◆ A quote or estimate on the costs involved.
◆ A timeline for completing the work.
◆ References and/or other supporting material.

Reality Check

Your follow-up letter is the first part of a proposal in which you feed back to Mr. Bigg his description of his situation exactly as he told it to you – without analysis, suggestions or solutions. This is why all those notes you took in the meeting are so important.

Wrap It Up and Take It Home

In the following endings from Traditional System thank you notes, it's clear that the applicants believe they are at the mercy of Mr. Bigg's whim, and are waiting for him to decide their fate:

"Once again, thank you for the opportunity to interview for a position with your company. If you require any additional information, please do not hesitate to contact me. Thank you for your time and consideration, and I look forward to hearing from you."

"I want to reiterate my strong interest in the position and in working with you and your staff. You provide the kind of opportunity I seek. Please call me at the telephone number above if I can provide you with any additional information."

"ABC Masters will be the ideal company to continue my career as a marketing professional. I will be available immediately to

begin work with your firm. I hope to hear from you soon."
"If you were to offer me this job, I believe that I could provide services that would meet the high standards of your corporation. Thank you for the interview and for your consideration, and I look forward to talking again with you."

Reality Check

The secret to writing an effective follow-up letter is to assume you have been hired because if you assume it, so will Mr. Bigg.

You don't get hired because you got lucky, somehow stumbled upon the right answers to a series of mind-numbing, nonsensical questions or beat your competition to mincemeat; you get hired because you have helped Mr. Bigg move himself from neutral to "yes."

Once Mr. Bigg realizes you can help him get what he wants, he will do everything he can to hire you.

The Clincher

Whatever you feel, believe or expect to happen as the result of a job interview will be expressed in your follow-up letter, and like it or not, thanks to the Law of Attraction, it will show up in your life.

If you have any doubts, concerns or fears at all about getting hired, you can count on your job search being filled with stalls, delays and lots of times coming real close, but rarely taking home the prize.

On the other hand, your absolute confidence that this job – or something better – is already yours will result in some very happy news very shortly.

Here's a Traditional System thank-you note from Monster.com with Mr. Bigg's responses in parentheses:

Did I Do All Right?

Thank you for the opportunity to discuss your opening for an auditor. I enjoyed meeting with you and learning more about Advantage Accounting, its current activities and upcoming projects.

(I'm glad you had fun. I'm still unpacking from a long business trip and wanted to put the meeting off for two weeks, but my secretary said you insisted on seeing me, even though it was very inconvenient for me. If we didn't have such an urgent need to hire someone, I wouldn't have bothered with you because you were so inconsiderate.)

I was very impressed with your strong commitment to innovation and employee satisfaction and productivity. Your volunteer program is a creative example of your company's belief that corporations should be vitally connected to their communities, a sentiment I wholeheartedly support. I would welcome the chance to be a part of this culture and work at your firm.

(Thanks for the nice words about our volunteer program, but I spent most of the meeting discussing our problems with integrating our various divisions to conform to our new accounting system. Since you didn't bother mentioning it, you must not have thought it too important.)

I believe my academic training and my experience working in the accounting department at LYP Jeans Company last summer qualify me for the position. In addition, my extensive knowledge of computer systems would be valuable as an auditor with your firm.

(What you believe is irrelevant; what matters is what I believe, and I believe I'm going to keep looking for someone else for this job.)

I look forward to hearing from you soon. In the meantime, please call me if I can provide more information or answer any additional questions.

(In about three weeks, you'll get a letter saying we've hired someone else.)

Score: I's: 12 You's: 10

Comments: By following the Traditional System, this potential candidate has alienated the very person she wants to work for. Her thank-you note is a weak attempt to flatter Mr. Bigg, and he isn't falling for it.

Here is the same applicant applying for the same job with the same company, but now her letter is written from Mr. Bigg's perspective about his needs, instead of trying to make her case.

Notice how the structure of this follow-up letter is similar to that of a Contrarian System cover letter, and pay special attention to the final paragraph.

This Could Be Good For Both Of Us

The Grabber

It was a real pleasure meeting with you yesterday. Given the many projects you are involved with, it's no wonder that you operate on a very tight schedule.

(And I really appreciate your patience and persistence. My secretary said you were cheerful and courteous, even though I had to cancel our meeting twice at the last minute. Now that I'm back and settled in from my trip, I can focus on hiring the right person for this job. Thanks for understanding.)

Recapping Mr. Bigg's problem

In our meeting, you described how Advantage Accounting is experiencing challenges in integrating the different accounting systems used by the many small firms you have acquired over the last few years into one universal system.

And of course, it's not just the technical issues involved here; the key to your on-going success will lie in ensuring that your employees embrace these changes through continuous training and motivation.

(You got our problem exactly right! You seem to have a grasp on the situation already, which will make things a whole lot easier as we move forward.)

Assuming the sale

John, I appreciate your specific concerns as you remain competitive, and I look forward to working with you and your associates in helping Advantage Accounting assert its rightful position as the country's top boutique accounting firm.

> (The office just down the hall from me is vacant; we'll put you in there for now until we can get you better quarters. What color do you want your furniture?)

> Score: I's: 2 You's: 14

Comments: This applicant already had the job in Mr. Bigg's mind when she left the interview, but this letter secured her future as his protégé.

Her letter projects low-keyed enthusiasm, combined with the confidence she will be hired – without being arrogant, pushy or trying to sell herself in any way. She didn't need to; Mr. Bigg gladly bought her instead.

CHAPTER SIXTEEN

It Ain't Over 'Til It's Over

*"Whatever we expect with confidence
becomes our own self-fulfilling prophecy."*

–Brian Tracy, Author

FINAL DETAILS

"Your only limitations are your own expectations."

– Janet White

My very first job out of college was as a writer for the in-house magazine of International Paper, so take it from me:

♦ Resume paper, resume stock and other special papers are merely marketing ploys by the paper companies, and are designed solely to part you from your money.

♦ If you think you need resume paper to get a job, then you believe the weight of your paper, rather than the weight of your words, is going to get you hired.

If you don't believe paper has magical qualities and just like using heavy weight stock, go get a ream of bond paper. But if you just want something to write on, use plain white copier paper. Mr. Bigg won't notice or care.

When you use snail mail for your initial contact with Mr. Bigg, spend the extra pennies and mail your materials flat in a 9" x 12" nonclasp, manila envelope. You want your materials to stay either on Mr. Bigg's desk or in his filing cabinet, and neither of those things will happen if your material has folds, no matter how good it is.

Draggin' The Line

Remember that list of up to 25 companies you developed back in the beginning of your job search? If you are at all concerned about using the Contrarian System, practice using it on the smaller companies at the bottom of your list.

As you use the Contrarian System, you will probably get offers of employment from some of these companies. Don't accept because you think there is a shortage of jobs and you're lucky to grab one; reread Chapter Two if you still believe this.

Smaller firms are a great place to start, especially if you're new to an industry, have little experience or few credentials, or are moving to an area where you have no or few contacts or connections.

Such companies nearly always have more work and/or opportunities than people to handle them, and they are often devoid of the limited thinking, internal bickering and rigid structure of larger companies.

Also, you'll be appreciated a whole lot more, have much more room for growth than you would at a larger company, and their money is just as green as anyone else's.

You Want to Do *What?*

Working for someone else isn't for everyone. If you have difficulty conforming to someone else's ideas of what you should do for a living, how you should do it, how far you should go, and how much you should make, the "security" of a paycheck may not be worth the grief.

When you work for someone else, they own you for the time they are paying you, and they have the legal right to take possession of everything you do that's work-related, even if you do it at home on your own time with your own resources. You may have thought of it, nurtured it, developed it and produced it, but don't expect to keep it because legally it's theirs.

Then there's always the possibility you'll be fired, let go, downsized, laid off, relocated, transferred or bored out of your mind at a dead-end job you've grown to hate. There is, in fact, no such thing as "job stability" when you have a job.

And some people, especially those who have reached the pinnacle of their professions, may find they are too good, too expensive or too high up in their careers to take a step down, so they become self-employed, typically as consultants.

For some, the decision to become their own boss can be overwhelming. While some people take to the entrepreneurial life with glee, others react with horror, and only the structured setting of a real job with a boss and a regular paycheck will do.

Stephen's Saga

"Stephen" was the executive vice president of the Dallas-based, multi-family division of a national commercial real estate company, heading one of the largest apartment portfolios in the country.

One day without warning, the company was sold to its largest competitor. The new owner was a mega-conglomerate with a large apartment portfolio, and already its own "Stephen" on board.

So while everyone else at the old company was hired to continue managing their properties, Stephen, who had managed the people who managed the properties, was given an extremely large check and told to have a nice life.

With his 25 years of experience and phenomenal track record, Stephen was an expert at what he did, and his future as a consultant was bright.

But Stephen saw himself as an employee (albeit a high-level one) who received a regular paycheck and was part of a chain of command, and he refused to consider any other option.

Stephen was firmly entrenched in the Traditional System, and assumed all it would take to get himself a new executive-level job in the apartment management industry would be to send his resume to a few headhunters, sit back and wait.

Much to his surprise, the pickings were lean. One headhunter recruited him for what turned out to be a senior-level sales job, which Stephen emphatically did not want to do. The others weren't interested in him, since their searches for the kind of position he wanted were few and far between.

Shortly after the layoff, Stephen was offered a job as a regional vice president at an apartment company in Chicago. It was a good company and the pay was more than fair, but this move would be a step down for Stephen because he used to manage regional vice presidents.

Stephen kept the offer as a fallback position because the company said they'd take him any time he wanted to join them. He was confident it wouldn't be long before he'd be back at work in an executive capacity.

One year after being let go, Stephen was still unemployed. With his ego bruised and his self-confidence shattered, he took the job in Chicago because it was the only offer he had. And the sad part was he felt he had to settle for whatever he could get.

Infinite Possibilities

It is essential for your personal growth and professional success that you turn a deaf ear to negative thinkers and "helpful" advice from people who don't know what they're talking about, regardless of who they are, what they think they know or how much credibility you think they have.

Steer clear of anyone who does not empower, encourage or uplift you in some way. When other people express their opinion about what you should or shouldn't do or think, remember that they are only seeing life through their own perspective, and expressing their inherent biases, fears and insecurities. Don't make their limitations yours.

Remember that the Law of Attraction is always creating demonstrations of your thoughts, feelings and beliefs, and whether it works in your life by default or design is entirely up to you.

Reality Check

The ultimate secret to getting your dream job or anything else you want in life is to know what you want, and to know beyond a shadow of a doubt that it is already yours. And so it is.

ADDENDUM

Breathe!

*"To be thrown upon one's own resources
is to be cast into the very lap of fortune."*

– Benjamin Franklin, American Statesman

FINISHING TOUCHES

*"What lies behind us and what lies before us
are tiny matters compared to what lies within us."*

– *Ralph Waldo Emerson*

The best advice I can give you if you want to get hired is to stop reading Traditional System books, articles or websites, or going to Traditional System classes and seminars on job hunting and resume writing. You've been there, done that – enough already!

And of course, don't read the want ads unless you are happily employed and want to see what's out there, learn what companies are in trouble, or need a good laugh.

Want ads in every form should be avoided if you have even the slightest hint of discontent on your job, or are planning to get hired within the next six months. Consider them poison.

Forget about using the web for finding employment; use it to find knowledge instead. Web surf effectively by going to sites that will teach you about your industry or the industry you want to be in, and the companies and people who are now in it. After all, you'll probably end up working with some of them.

Most importantly, there are thousands of websites, books and courses on how to use the incredible power of the Universe that is already within you to get the job of your dreams, improve your health, turn around your financial situation, have loving, rewarding relationships and bring you your heaven on earth.

For when you change your thinking, you change your life.

Do the Hustle – Not

I suggest you also read books and websites that will teach you the basics of professional, business-to-business selling, which you now know has nothing to do with the Traditional System form of pitching and hustling.

Even if you are not going into selling for a living, you still sell all the time. When you persuade someone to change their mind about something or to agree with you, you have made a "sale" because they have moved themselves from neutral or "no" to "yes."

In particular, you might want to get some of the books on selling recommended below. In the late 1970's when women first moved into the corporate world, to everyone's astonishment, they consistently outsold men.

It shouldn't have been a surprise; women instinctively teach and persuade, which tends to attract people, and men tend to pitch and hustle, which tends to alienate people. It would do many men a world of good to learn how to sell like a woman, especially if they want to get hired.

Some of these books are out of print, but you can find them or others like them on e-bay, HalfPriceBooks.com, Amazon.com, and at library book fairs, garage sales, etc.

Others have been reprinted and updated, and new ones are published all the time. The books and websites I recommend the most are listed first, but they're all good.

SUGGESTED READING LIST

Money
Free e-books
- Accept Your Abundance,
  www.prosperitypowerexperience.com
- The Science of Getting Rich,
  www.scienceofgettingrich.net

Most Recommended
- *The Dynamic Laws of Prosperity*, Catherine Ponder
- *Think and Grow Rich*, Napoleon Hill
- *Think Yourself Rich*, Joseph Murphy and Ian McMahan

Highly Suggested
- *Breaking the Money Barriers*, Michael Duckett
- *The Abundance Book*, John Randolph Price
- *The Four Spiritual Laws of Prosperity: A Simple Guide to Unlimited Abundance*, Edwene Gaines
- *The Wealthy Spirit: Daily Affirmations for Financial Stress Reduction*, Chellie Campbell
- *Wealth 101: Getting What You Want/Enjoying What You've Got*, John-Roger & Peter McWilliams

Motivation/Self-Improvement
Free e-books
- www.universallawastoday.com
- www.newthoughtlibrary.com

Most Recommended
- *Creative Visualization*, Shakti Gawain
- *Dare to Be Great: Seven Steps to Spiritual and Material Riches*, Terry Cole-Whittaker
- *Directing the Movies of Your Mind*, Adelaide Bry
- *Discover the Power Within You*, Eric Butterworth
- *Row, Row, Row Your Boat: A Guide for Living In the Divine Flow*, Steven Lane Taylor

- *See You At the Top,* Zig Ziglar
- *The Cosmic Power Within You,* Joseph Murphy
- *The Hell I Can't!,* Terry McBride
- *The Magic of Thinking Big,* David Schwartz
- *The Power of Positive Thinking,* Norman Vincent Peale
- *The Power of Your Subconscious Mind,* Joseph Murphy & Ian McMahan
- *The Science of Mind,* Ernest Holmes
- "The Secret" DVD, www.thesecret.tv

Highly Suggested
- *How to Stop Worrying and Start Living,* Dale Carnegie
- *Peace of Mind Through Possibility Thinking,* Robert Schuller
- *The Magic of Getting What You Want,* David Schwartz
- *The Wisdom of Florence Scovel Shinn,* Florence Scovel Shinn
- *What to Say When You Talk to Yourself,* Shad Helmstetter
- *You Can If You Think You Can,* Norman Vincent Peale
- *Your Best Life Now: Seven Steps to Living at Your Full Potential,* Joel Olsteen

Negotiating/Selling
Most Recommended
- *The Best Way in the World for a Woman to Make Money,* David King and Karen Levine
- *The Secrets of Super Selling,* Lynea Corson, George Hadley, Carl Stevens
- *You Can Get Anything You Want (But You Have to Do More than Ask),* Roger Dawson

Highly Suggested
- *Getting to Yes: Negotiating Agreement Without Giving In,* Roger Fisher & William Ury
- *Negotiate to Close: How to Make More Successful Deals,* Gary Karrass
- *Saleswoman,* Barbara Pletcher
- *Selling is a Woman's Game,* Nicki Joy & Susan Kane-Benson
- *The Woman's New Selling Game,* Carole Hyatt

How to Manifest Your Dream Job (Or Anything Else!)

By Janet White

Know What You Want And That It's Now Yours

Create a mental video of yourself at work in your dream job:

- What are you doing, wearing or reading? What does your work place look like?
- How much money are you making? What is your work schedule?
- Who are your co-workers?
- How do you feel doing this work in this environment with these people?

Replay this mental video several times a day, and especially right before you go to sleep, until your dream job shows up.

Know that this job is yours right now; even if you can't yet see it, haven't a clue how it will come to you or if it seems impossible.

Be Who You Now Are

The fastest way to manifest your dream job is to think, speak and act as if you already have it:

- Have a business card printed specifying the kind of work you see yourself doing.
- Attend trade functions and mingle with your peers.
- Take classes and seminars and read industry publications.
- Keep your mind filled with thoughts of how great it is to do the work you love.
- Use affirmations and visualizations to intentionally reprogram your mind to accept you now have your dream job.

Never allow fear, doubt, misgivings or anyone else's opinions to sway you from your conviction that what you want is already yours. Negative thoughts will block or delay it from coming to you.

Do What Feels Right

Embrace the "knowing" and embody the "being," and you'll be intuitively guided to take the most appropriate actions towards your goal.

Relax; you won't have to "do" very much at all, and what you do will be exceptionally productive. Step out in faith, and your dream job will manifest at the perfect time and in the perfect way for your highest good.

Stop trying to "make it happen" or worrying how it will show up. Knowing what you want and expecting to receive it is your job; how the Universe's gets it to you is not your concern.

You attract whatever you focus on, so focus only on what you want, not on what you don't want. Either way, it's already on its way to you.

THE LAW OF ATTRACTION

Ask and it shall be given to you; seek and you shall find;

knock and it shall be opened to you.

It is done unto you as you believe.

As within, so without.

Thoughts are things.

If you believe it, you will see it.

For whoever has, to him will more be given, and he who does not have, even that which he has will be taken from him.

As a man thinketh, so is he.

Change your thinking and change your life.